The SIMS
HOUSE PARTY
EXPANSION PACK

PRIMA'S OFFICIAL STRATEGY GUIDE

MARK COHEN

Prima Games
A Division of Prima Communications, Inc.
3000 Lava Ridge Court
Roseville, CA 95661
(916) 787-7000
www.primagames.com

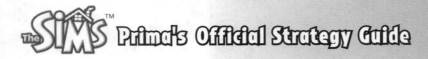

Senior Product Manager: Jennifer Croutteau
Senior Project Editor: Christy L. Curtis
Editorial Assistant: Terri Stewart

Important:

ISBN: 7615-3549-7

Library of Congress Catalog Card Number: 2001088971

Printed in the United States of America

01 02 03 04 BB 10 9 8 7 6 5 4 3 2 1

Acknowledgments

Playing *The Sims* for hours tends to blur the line between reality and fantasy, but fortunately I had the assistance of the Prima publishing team to keep me on track. A special thank you to Jennifer Crotteau, Christy Curtis, and Terri Stewart Bloom. To Asha Johnson, thank you for your timely copy editing assistance. Kudos to David Chong, who partied hearty to supply the strategies and tips for the *House Party* section.

Prima thanks everyone at Maxis for their assistance, namely: Tim LeTourneau, Emily Kenner, Jenna Chalmers, Kevin O'Hare, Waylon Wilsonoff, Kyle Brink, and Kimberly Ferrara.

Contents

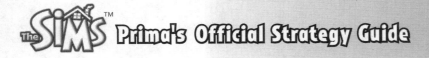

INTRODUCTION:
HOW TO USE THIS BOOK

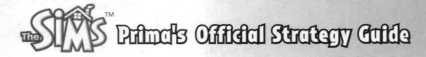

Introduction

Trying to distill the essence of *The Sims* into a strategy guide is in many ways an impossible task. Unlike traditional computer games that have a beginning, a middle, and an end, *The Sims* only has a middle. Once you get used to your characters and their world, the game settles into a never-ending adventure that is limited only by your imagination, or your capacity for the absurd, whichever comes first. The faster you start fiddling with your Sims' lives—for better or for worse—the sooner you'll experience the wonder of this game, so without further ado, here's what to expect in the following pages.

Part I: *The Sims*

The guide is split into two parts: *The Sims* (chapters 1–10) and *The Sims: House Party Expansion Pack* (chapters 11–15). Chapter 1, "What's Your Sim Sign?", explains how a Sim thinks, acts, and reacts in various situations. At the beginning of the game, you can mold your Sims' basic personalities, and we tell you how these traits will affect their lives.

Chapter 2, "Motives—I Want, I Need; Therefore, I Am a Sim!", explains the eight primal urges that drive all Sims. We cover each one in detail, and then blend the information with the previous chapter, so that you begin to understand how a Sim's actions can be manipulated by you, and by other Sims.

Sims are very social creatures, and this can be a blessing or a curse. Chapter 3, "Interacting with Other Sims," shows you how and why a Sim interacts with others, and explains the benefits and pitfalls that accompany friendships, love relationships, and children.

Chapter 4, "9 to 5—Climbing the Career Ladder," looks at the working life of a Sim. You have myriad career choices and opportunities for advancement, and we provide you with the tools to get the job and promotions that will make your Sim financially successful.

Chapter 5, "Building a House," has building tutorials that take you through every step of the construction process, from putting up the framing to slapping on the final coat of paint. Our topics include walls, windows, doors, wall coverings, stairways and second stories, pools, and landscaping.

A Sim home is empty until you fill it with lots of stuff. Chapter 6, "Material Sims," provides facts and statistics on every single object you can buy, more than 150 items in all. In addition to data and descriptions, we use detailed lists and tables to show how items relate to each other, and how some objects can even alter the effectiveness of other objects.

Now, it's time to put everything you know into action. We devote chapter 7, "All in the Family," and to describing the common and not-so-common events in a Sim's life. Get ready for a wild ride as we give you insights on single life, relationships, having children, and making friends.

Chapter 8, "A Day in the Life," follows a few of our families as they handle the ups and downs fo Sim life. Check it out to see examples of our Sims in interesting situations.

Chapter 9, "Sim Survival Tips," is a quick-reference guide for times of crisis. Simply turn to the appropriate Motive and save your Sim's life with one of our game-tested tips. Or, if you're feeling devious, check out our cheats to satisfy your Sim's needs.

We finish up with chapter 10, "Extending Your World." Find suggestions for extending your Sim environment with special utilities and third party creations. You won't believe how many people are hooked on this game, and you'll be amazed at the thousands of new skins, heads, objects, homes, and wallpapers available to you...absolutely free on dozens of *Sim* websites.

Part II: *House Party Expansion Pack*

So much for the original *Sims* game. By now you have your Sims leading typically abnormal lives and you're ready for something different. You came to the right chapters.

Chapter 11, "New Toys," provides complete tables listing every new item's purchase price, related Motives, and Efficiency ratings. Use this chapter to make informed decisions about what to buy to fulfill your Sims' needs within their budget.

Chapters 12, "Sim Party Animals," includes comprehensive coverage of the all-new *House Party* characters, including Entertainer, Caterer, Psycho Mime, and Campfire Ghost.

Chapter 13, "Setting the Mood," goes over the ground rules, with tips on planning every aspect of your "House Party," including party objects, house planning, and decor.

Chapter 14, "House Party Neighborhoods," will help you make the most of your multiple neighborhoods, manage families, and import houses like a land-developing master.

Chapter 15, "Let's Party," shows you how to get a party started, kick it into high gear, and keep it humming long enough to inspire a few special guests to show up.

There you have it, the ultimate *Sims* and *House Party* resource. Now, go out and get crazy with the number-one computer game of all time; and remember, be kind to your Sims (at least some of the time, anyway).

PART I:

The SIMS™

CHAPTER 1:
WHAT'S YOUR SIM SIGN?

Introduction

When you are charged with the solemn task of creating a Sim from scratch, you have 25 points to distribute over five traits: Neat, Outgoing, Active, Playful, and Nice. Whether we admit it or not, all of us have an inherent wish to be perfectly balanced people (or Sims). Of course, you can take the easy way out and award five points in every category, creating a generic Sim. You'll spend less time managing a middle-of-the-road Sim because in most situations, he or she will do the right thing. If you'd rather play it safe, skip this chapter and move right to "Motives: I Want…I Need…Therefore, I Am a Sim". If not, read on as we describe the subtle (and sometimes dramatic) outcomes that your personality ratings will inspire.

It's in the Stars

As you play with the personality bars, you'll note the changing zodiac sign that appears on the screen. Of course, a serious astrologer would argue that a true personality profile is based on much more than five traits. However, if you have a basic understanding of newspaper horoscopes, you'll be able to recognize yourself, or someone close to you, as you create a Sim personality. In the next section we'll look at each trait and examine the potential effects of your ratings in various game situations. But first, let's take a look at basic interpersonal compatibility as seen through the eyes of the zodiac. The following table gives you the best and worst matchups for friends and lovers. This doesn't necessarily imply that any other Relationship outside of the table is doomed; it is merely an indication of how hard you'll have to work on it.

Sims Zodiac Compatibility Table

SIGN	ATTRACTED TO	REPELLED BY
Aries	Gemini/Taurus	Cancer/Libra
Taurus	Aries/Libra	Virgo/Cancer
Gemini	Pisces/Virgo	Capricorn/Aries
Cancer	Taurus/Scorpio	Gemini/Aries
Virgo	Aquarius/Sagittarius	Leo/Taurus
Libra	Virgo/Cancer	Pisces/Scorpio
Scorpio	Pisces/Leo	Libra/Aquarius
Sagittarius	Pisces/Capricorn	Libra/Scorpio
Leo	Sagittarius/Cancer	Capricorn/Gemini
Capricorn	Aquarius/Taurus	Leo/Gemini
Aquarius	Capricorn/Sagittarius	Scorpio/Virgo
Pisces	Scorpio/Gemini	Leo/Aries

Personality Traits

The following sections review what you can expect from each type of Sim, with examples of how different personality traits will manifest during the game. For our purposes, we'll divide the ratings bar into three sections: Low (1–3), Average (4–7), and High (8–10). These numbers correspond to the number of light blue bars to the right of each trait.

Neat

Low

Don't expect these Sims to pick up their dirty dishes, wash their hands after using the bathroom, or take timely showers. They are perfectly content to let others clean up their messes.

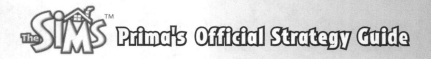

Fig. 1-1. The kitchen floor is a perfect place for this messy Sim's snack leavings.

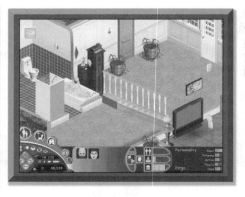

Fig. 1-3. This fastidious Sim goes straight to the bathtub after a hard day's work.

Medium

At least these Sims keep themselves relatively clean, and you can depend on them to clean up their own messes. Occasionally they'll even clean up another Sim's garbage, but you might have to intervene if you have several cleanup items that need attention.

Fig. 1-2. After slopping water all over the bathroom during his shower, this moderately neat Sim mops up his mess before leaving the room.

Outgoing

Low

Shy, reserved, Sims have less pressing needs for Social interaction, so it will be more difficult to pursue friendships with other Sims, although they can still carry on stimulating conversations. Within their own home, a shy Sim may be less interested in receiving hugs, kisses, and back rubs, so if you are looking for romance, it would be a good idea to find a compatible target (see zodiac chart on p. 2).

Fig. 1-4. This Sim cringes at the thought of a back rub—poor guy.

High

A super-neat Sim always checks the vicinity for dirty dishes and old newspapers, and of course, personal hygiene is a big priority. One of these Sims can compensate for one or two slobs in a household.

Medium

It will be a little easier to get this Sim to mix with strangers and enjoy a little intimacy from his housemates. Don't expect a party animal, but you'll be able to entice your guests into most activities.

Fig. 1-5. Come on everyone, let's hit the pool!

High

This Sim needs plenty of Social stimulation to prevent his or her Social score from plummeting. You'll have no trouble throwing parties or breaking the ice with just about any personality type.

Fig. 1-6. This outgoing Sim is still unconscious from last night's pool party, and she has inspired the close friendship of another man. Hmmm.

Active

Low

Forget about pumping iron or swimming 100 laps at 5:00 a.m. These Sims prefer a soft easy chair to a hard workout. A sofa and a good TV are high on their priority list. In fact, if they don't get their daily ration of vegging, their Comfort scores will suffer.

Fig. 1-7. This Sim says "No way!" to a session on the exercise bench.

Medium

These Sims strike a good balance between relaxing and breaking a sweat. They dance, swim, and even shoot hoops without expressing discomfort.

Fig. 1-8. His Active rating is only a four, but that doesn't stop this Sim from shooting hoops in his jammies.

High

Active Sims like to pick up the pace rather than fall asleep on the sofa in front of the TV. Get these Sims a pool, basketball hoop, or exercise bench, and plan on dancing the night away with friends.

Fig. 1-9. Even in her business suit, this active Sim will gladly leave Mortimer on the sofa and pump some iron in the backyard.

Medium

These well-rounded Sims are usually receptive to a good joke and don't mind a little tickling. They may not be the first ones on the dance floor, but they'll join in with a good crowd.

Fig. 1-11. This Sim is Playful enough to dance, even though she is overdue for a shower.

Playful

Low

Get these Sims a bookcase, a comfortable chair, and plenty of books. If reading isn't an option, looking at a painting or playing a game of chess will do just fine.

Fig. 1-10. There's always time to watch the fish, for this less-than-playful Sim.

High

Can you spell P-A-R-T-Y? These Sims love to have a few drinks, dance to good music, and invite lots of guests over to the house. They love telling jokes, and they are usually ready to laugh at others' stories.

Fig. 1-12. This Playful kid would get the Maid in the pool for a game of chicken, if only she would respond.

Nice

Low

There is nothing redeeming about a grouchy Sim. They are always ready to tease or insult their friends, and they love to brag. A Sim with a low Nice rating should be dropped from your guest list immediately, or asked to leave if he or she shows up.

Fig. 1-13. Usually a compliment elicits a nice response, but not so with with sourpuss.

Medium

This Sim keeps an even keel about most things. Of all the traits, Nice is the least destructive if you award at least four points. Only the nastiest Sims can get under a medium-Nice Sim's skin.

Fig. 1-14. This Sim has time for a good tickle, even while mopping up the bathroom.

High

These Sims just want to make the world a better place for everyone. If there was a Sim beauty contest, the winner would be extremely "Nice."

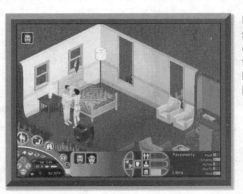

Fig. 1-15. Even after spending the night on the kitchen floor, this Sim still knows how to compliment her mate.

Personality Tables

The following tables demonstrate how personality traits affect Fun scores and Skill development.

Traits that Raise Max Fun Value

PERSONALITY TRAIT	RAISES MAX FUN SCORE FOR
Playful	Aquarium, Chess Table, Computer, Doll House, Flamingo, Pinball, TV (Cartoon Channel), VR Glasses
Serious (Low Playful)	Newspaper (Read)
Active	Basketball Hoop, Play Structure, TV (Action Channel)
Outgoing	Hot Tub, TV (Romance Channel)
Grouchy (Low Nice)	TV (Horror Channel)

Skills Accelerated by Personality

SKILL	OBJECTS USED TO INCREASE SKILL	TRAIT ACCELERATOR
Creativity	Easel, Piano	Playful
Body	Exercise Machine, Swimming Pool	Active
Charisma	Medicine Cabinet, Mirrors	Outgoing

CHAPTER 2:
MOTIVES—I WANT, I NEED; THEREFORE, I AM A SIM!

CHAPTER 2: MOTIVES—I WANT, I NEED; THEREFORE, I AM A SIM!

Introduction

When you consider how many needs, traits, and desires make up a Sim's personality, it would be an injustice to call it AI. Never before has a computer-generated character interacted so completely with both the game and the gamer while maintaining a unique (and ever-changing) personality. Is it any wonder that *The Sims* has topped the PC sales chart for nearly two years running?

In the previous chapter we discussed a Sim's personality traits. It painted a broad picture of the various types of Sims you might encounter in the game, much the same as a newspaper horoscope tells a superficial story of a person's life. In this chapter, we advance from broad-brush personality traits to the eight powerful Motives that drive a Sim's every action. We cover each Motive in detail, but first, let's begin with a few basic definitions.

What Is a Motive?

A Motive is, very simply, a need. Your Sims follow these needs, based on their own instincts and a little help from you. If you activate Free Will in the Options menu, your Sims will also make their own decisions, based on changing needs. After selecting a Motive to fulfill, be it Hunger or Hygiene, the Sim is "rewarded" with Motive points. These points raise the corresponding Motive score.

The eight Motive scores are displayed on the right side of the control panel. A Motive rating is considered positive if the bar is green, and negative if it is red. Internally, the game uses a 200-point system, with positive (green) ratings between 0 and 100, and negative (red) ratings from 0 to -100.

> **TIP**
> When any of the Sims' eight Motives drop below a certain level, a Sim will cease an activity that doesn't improve the Motive in distress. So, you'll see low-priority items drop out of the activity queue, or your Sim will add an activity that addresses the critical need.

> **CAUTION**
> Without Free Will, your Sims depend entirely on your input to keep them alive. If you don't tell them to eat, they will starve, and eventually die.

Mood Rating

The game control panel also displays a Mood Rating, just to the right of the Sim character icons. If the rating is positive, you see up to five green bars displayed above the comedy/tragedy masks. When the Mood Rating is negative, it displays up to five red bars below the masks.

In calculating the Mood Rating, each of the eight Motives is weighted, based on how critical it is to sustaining a Sim's life. Hence, Hunger, Bladder, and Energy, which are all related to a Sim's physical well-being, carry more weight than the noncritical Motives such as Social, Fun, or Room. So, if a Sim is hungry and tired, as pictured in figure 2-1, the overall Mood Rating will be relatively low, even if several other Motives are high.

Fig. 2-1. This Sim kid's overall Mood Rating is barely positive, due to the fact that he is starving and low on Energy.

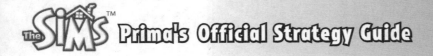

The Motives

In the following sections we describe the eight Motives, using several tables to show you how and why a Sim reacts to different objects in the environment. By recognizing the relationships between Motives and objects, you'll begin to understand how a Sim considers a perpetual barrage of options. Once you do this, the only remaining question is, "Who is really in charge here, you or the Sim?"

Fig. 2-2. This Sim family enjoys a meal together. Mom's Hunger bar is in the worst shape, so she has a second meal plate at the ready.

Aside from the overall Motive weighting system, each Sim suffers different rates of Motive depreciation based on personality traits. For example, a Playful Sim must have more "rewards" to maintain the Fun Motive bar. Similarly, an Outgoing Sim requires more interaction with other Sims to maintain the Social score.

Hunger Score for Each Meal, Snack, or Gift

MEAL TYPE	HUNGER MOTIVE BAR POINTS
Snack	9
Quick Meal	16
Full Meal	16
Group Meal (per serving)	16
Pizza (per serving)	33
Candy Box (gift)	3 (per serving, 12 servings per box)
Fruitcake (gift)	7 (per slice, 6 slices per box)

Hunger

For obvious reasons, a Sim cannot survive for very long without food. We'll cover the details of food preparation in a later chapter, but for now let's focus on the basics. As long as you have a refrigerator, a Sim can enjoy a Snack, Quick Meal, Full Meal, or Group Meal (same as a Full Meal, except one of the Sims prepares several servings). In addition to preparing food, a Sim with a telephone can order out for Pizza, or enjoy food that was brought as a gift (Candy Box or Fruitcake). The Hunger Motive bar points awarded with each meal are outlined in the following table.

Comfort

The next category listed in the Needs section of the control panel is considerably less important than Hunger. Sims like to be comfortable, and they love cushy chairs, oversized sofas, and supportive beds. Spending more money on these objects translates into greater Motive rewards. However, if your budget is tight, you must still furnish the house with basic furniture or your Sims will express their discomfort.

Fig. 2-3. With only a cheap chair and loveseat, this Sim's Comfort score is mired in the red.

Fig. 2-4. Three out of four Motive scores are on the way up while this couple enjoys a hot tub soak.

Hunger, Bladder, Energy, and Comfort are the most demanding of Motives, because if any one score drops below a certain level, the Sim will immediately exit his or her current activity to remedy the deficit. The following table lists the exit triggers for each category.

Mandatory Exit Factors

MOTIVE	SIM TYPE	EXITS CURRENT INTERACTION WHEN MOTIVE DROPS BELOW
Bladder	Resident	-85
Bladder	Visitor	-80
Comfort	Resident	-90
Comfort	Visitor	-60
Energy	Resident	-80
Energy	Visitor	-70
Hunger	Resident	-80
Hunger	Visitor	-40

Hygiene

Bad Hygiene will never kill a Sim, although it may seriously gross out others in the immediate vicinity. Solving this problem is easy—have your Sims wash their hands or take a shower. You can also combine Hygiene with other Motives. Taking a bath boosts the Hygiene and Comfort scores, while a soak in the hot tub (with friends) rewards the Hygiene, Comfort, Social, and Fun Motive bars.

Bladder

If you can't satisfy the Bladder urge, you'll be cleaning up puddles on the floor. Just make sure you find a bathroom before the Motive bar turns full red. A Sloppy Sim creates an additional risk by not regularly flushing the toilet. If you don't issue timely reminders, the toilet could get clogged, causing a major mess.

Pay special attention to the Bladder bar when your Sim spends time at the Beverage Bar or drinks a lot of coffee.

The Hygiene score takes a nose dive if a Sim can't get to the bathroom in time and pees on the floor.

Fig. 2-5. This Sim's Bladder is not quite full, but unless his guest vacates the bathroom soon, he could be in trouble.

Energy

We're talking sleep, pure and simple. Ideally, a good night's sleep should turn the bar completely green. This will happen at varying rates, depending upon the quality of the mattress, so you can get by on less sleep if you splurge for an expensive bed. If your Sim can't get to the bedroom or a couch before the Energy bar turns completely red, the floor becomes your only option. If this happens, wake your Sim and find the closest bed. A night on the hard floor will degrade your Sim's Comfort level to zero, while only restoring partial energy.

If your Sim stays up too late playing computer games, a shot of espresso provides a temporary Energy boost, although it will also fill the Bladder at an increased rate. Espresso has a powerful effect, but it takes longer to consume, which could be a problem if the car pool driver is honking.

Fig. 2-6. It never hurts to send your kids to bed early, because if they are tired in the morning, a coffee jolt is not an option.

Fun

Sims like to cut loose from the daily grind and have Fun, but depending upon their personalities, they prefer different activities. For example, a Playful Sim leans toward computer games, pinball machines, and train sets; while a more Serious Sim would rather sit down to a quiet game of chess or spend a few minutes gazing at a painting.

Fig. 2-7. These two Sims enjoy a game of pool after work.

Kids need to have more Fun than adults, and the effects of a single play session deteriorate faster for kids than for their older counterparts. Hence, it is a good idea to fill the house with plenty of juvenile diversions if you have children.

There are four different types of Fun activities: Extended, One-Time, Timed, and Endless. The following lists and tables provide additional information, including exit factors, for these pursuits.

Extended Fun Activities

Sims exit the following extended activities after reaching the maximum Fun score for their personality types. Hence, a Playful, Active Sim will stay on the basketball court longer than a Serious Sim.

- **Basketball Hoop**
- **Bookshelf (reading)**
- **Dollhouse**
- **Computer (playing games)**
- **Pinball Machine**
- **Play Structure**
- **Stereo**
- **Toy Box**
- **Train Set**
- **TV**
- **VR Glasses**

One-Time Fun Activities

The following activities raise a Sim's Fun score once with each interaction. It may take several interactions with the same activity for a Sim to reach the maximum Fun level.

OBJECT	ACTION
Aquarium	Feed or watch fish
Baby	Play
Diving Board	Dive into the pool
Espresso Machine	Drink espresso
Fountain	View
Lava Lamp	View
Painting	View
Sculpture	View

Timed (Pre-set) Fun Activities

As with the one-time activities listed above, a Sim may need to repeat the following activities to achieve maximum Fun points.

- **Chess Set**
- **Pool Table**

Endless Fun

- **Hot Tub:** A Sim will stay in the tub until Fun, Comfort, Social, and Hygiene numbers reach maximum levels.
- **Swimming Pool:** A Sim will keep doing laps until another Motive takes effect, or until you assign him or her to another activity.

Social

Sims crave other Sims, especially if they are Outgoing. Although they won't die without socializing, it is a good idea to devote a portion of each day to a group activity, even if it is a simple hot tub session with your Sim's mate, or a family meal.

Fig. 2-8. A casual conversation during breakfast raises this Sim's Social score.

The following table summarizes all of the possible Social interactions between adults and children. We take this one step further in the next chapter, "Interacting with Other Sims," where we examine Relationships.

Adult-Child Interactions

ACTION	ADULT TO ADULT	CHILD TO CHILD	ADULT TO CHILD	CHILD TO ADULT
Apologize	X	—	—	—
Attack	X	X	—	—
Brag	X	X	X	X
Call Here	X	X	X	X
Cheer Up	X	X	X	X
Compliment	X	—	—	—
Dance	X	—	—	—
Entertain	X	X	X	X
Flirt	X	—	—	—
Give Back Rub	X	—	—	—
Give Gift	X	X	X	X
Hug	X	X	X	X
Insult	X	X	X	X
Joke	X	X	X	X
Kiss	X	—	—	—
Say Goodbye	X	X	X	—
Scare	X	X	X	X
Slap	X	—	—	—
Tag	—	X	—	—
Talk	X	X	X	X
Tease	X	X	X	X
Tickle	X	X	X	X

Social Outcome Modifiers

You didn't expect a Sim Social encounter to be simple, did you? When one Sim communicates with another, several calculations determine the outcome. Factors include age (adult or child), sex, mood, and personality traits, not to mention the current state of their Relationship. Also, a Sim with strong Social needs (but few friends) may expect more from an encounter with a Sim who has similar needs.

The following table lists the factors that govern the choices that appear on a Social actions menu. For example, two Sims who are strangers are not likely to have the options to kiss or hug. Additionally, the table lists key factors that determine the eventual outcome.

rel = Relationship
out = Outgoing
play = Playful
ff = Friend Flag
ss = Same Sex
rom = Romance Flag
age = Adult/Child
social = Social Motive Value
vis = Visitor
budget = Household Budget
nice = Nice
body = Body

Social Outcome Factors

INTERACTION	FACTORS THAT DETERMINE APPEARANCE ON THE MENU	FACTORS THAT DETERMINE OUTCOME
Apologize	rel	mood
Attack	age, nice, mood, rel	body
Back Rub	age, nice, mood, rel, out, ss	rel, out, ss
Brag	nice, out, social, rel	rel, mood
Cheer Up	ff, mood (of friend), nice	rel
Compliment	age, nice, out, mood, rel	rel, mood
Dance	age, mood, out, rel	rel, out, mood
Entertain	social, out, play, mood, rel	play, rel
Flirt	age, social, ss, out, mood, rel, rom	rel, mood, ss
Gift	vis, budget, nice, mood, rel	rel, mood
Hug	age, out, mood, rel, ss	rel, out, mood, ss
Insult	nice, mood, rel	nice
Joke	play, mood, rel	play, mood, rel
Kiss	ss, mood, rel, age	rel, mood, ss
Scare	nice, mood, play, rel	play, mood
Slap	age, nice, mood, rel	nice, mood
Talk	mood, rel, out	topics match
Tease	nice, mood, rel	rel, mood
Tickle	social, out, play, active, mood, rel	rel, play

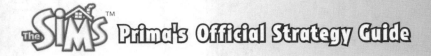
Room

This is a combined rating that analyzes the design and contents of the current room, and translates it into a Room score. Of all the Motives, Room is the least important. However, if you love your Sim, you'll want to create the best possible environment. The most important contributing factors to Room score are:

- **Light:** Sims hate dark rooms, so fill your house with sunlight (windows and paned doors), lamps, and wall lights.
- **Room Size:** Don't cramp your Sims into tiny rooms.
- **Corners:** As mentioned in the "Building a House" chapter, Sims love corners.
- **State of Repair:** Any items that are not functioning properly detract from the Room score (see following list).

Fig. 2-9. Who wouldn't love a kitchen like this? It's bright, roomy, nicely furnished, and packed with high-tech appliances.

Negative Impact on Room Score

- **Trash**
- **Floods**
- **Dirty plates**
- **Meals with flies**
- **Full trash cans/compactors**
- **Dead plants**
- **Puddle or ash pile**
- **Dead fish in aquariums**
- **Dirty objects (shower, toilet, tub)**

The following table lists the positive or negative value of every object in *The Sims*.

Room Score

OBJECT	STATE/TYPE	ROOM SCORE
Aquarium	Fish Alive	25
	Dirty	-25
	Dirty and/or Dead	-50
Ash	N/A	-10
Bar	N/A	20
Bed	Unmade (Any Bed)	-10
	Made Mission	30
	Made (Other than Mission)	10
Chair	Parisienne	25
	Empress	10
Clock (Grandfather)	N/A	50
Computer	Broken	-25
Counter	Barcelona	15
Desk	Redmond	15
Dresser	Antique Armoire	20
	Oak Armoire	10
Fire	N/A	-100

OBJECT	STATE/TYPE	ROOM SCORE
Fireplace	Library Edition (No Fire)	20
	Library Edition (Fire)	75
	Worcestershire (No Fire)	15
	Worcestershire (Fire)	60
	Bostonian (No Fire)	10
	Bostonian (Fire)	45
	Modesto (No Fire)	5
	Modesto (Fire)	30
Flamingo	N/A	10
Flood	N/A	-25
Flowers (Outdoor)	Healthy	20
	Dead	-20
Flowers/Plants (Indoor)	Healthy	10
	Wilted	0
	Dead	-10
Food	Snack (Spoiled)	-15
	Fruitcake (Empty Plate)	-5
	BBQ Group Meal (Spoiled)	-20
	BBQ Single Meal (Spoiled)	-15
	Empty Plate	-10
	Pizza Slice (Spoiled)	-10
	Pizza Box (Spoiled)	-25
	Candy (Spoiled)	-5
	Group Meal (Spoiled)	-20
	Meal (Spoiled)	-25
	Quick Meal (Spoiled)	-20
Fountain	N/A	25
Flowers (Gift)	Dead	-10
	Alive	20
Lamp	Not Broken	10
Lava Lamp	N/A	20
Newspaper	Old Newspapers	-20
Piano	N/A	30

OBJECT	STATE/TYPE	ROOM SCORE
Pinball Machine	Broken	-15
Shower	Broken	-15
Sofa (Deiter or Dolce)	N/A	20
Stereo	Strings	25
Table	Mesa	15
	Parisienne	25
Toilet	Clogged	-10
Train Set	Small	25
Trash Can (Inside)	Full	-20
Trash Compactor	Full	-25
Trash Pile	N/A	-20
TV	Soma	20
	Broken (Any TV)	-15

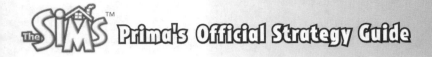 

Object Advertising Values

Earlier in the chapter we mentioned that Sims receive Motive rewards when they select an activity. If you are in complete control of your Sims (Free Will is off), you determine their choices. However, with Free Will on, Sims constantly poll their surroundings to compare which objects are "advertising" the most attractive rewards. The following table includes a Motive profile of every object in *The Sims*.

Object Advertising Values

OBJECT TYPE	POSSIBLE INTERACTIONS	OBJECT VARIATIONS	ADVERTISED MOTIVE	ADVERTISED VALUE	PERSONALITY TRAIT MODIFIER	REDUCED EFFECTS (OVER DISTANCE)
Aquarium	Clean & Restock	N/A	Room	30	Neat	Medium
	Feed Fish	N/A	Room	10	Nice	High
		N/A	Fun	10	Playful	High
	Watch Fish	N/A	Fun	10	Playful	High
Ash	Sweep Up	N/A	Energy	23	N/A	Medium
		N/A	Room	50	Neat	Medium
Baby	Play	N/A	Fun	50	Playful	Medium
Bar	Have Drink	N/A	Room	30	N/A	Low
	Grill	Barbecue	Energy	-10	N/A	Low
			Hunger	40	Cooking	Low
Basketball Hoop	Join	N/A	Fun	30	Active	High
		N/A	Social	20	N/A	Medium
		N/A	Energy	-20	N/A	Medium
	Play	N/A	Fun	30	Active	High
		N/A	Energy	-20	N/A	High
Bed	Make Bed	All Beds	Room	25	Neat	High
	Sleep	Double Bed (Cheap Eazzzzze)	Energy	65	N/A	None
		Double Bed (Napoleon)	Energy	67	N/A	None
		Double Bed (Mission)	Energy	70	N/A	None
		Single Bed (Spartan)	Energy	60	N/A	None
		Single Bed (Tyke Nyte)	Energy	63	N/A	None
	Tuck in Kid	All Beds	Energy	160	Nice	None

OBJECT TYPE	POSSIBLE INTERACTIONS	OBJECT VARIATIONS	ADVERTISED MOTIVE	ADVERTISED VALUE	PERSONALITY TRAIT MODIFIER	REDUCED EFFECTS (OVER DISTANCE)
Bookcase	Read a Book	Bookcase (Pine)	Fun	10	Serious	High
		Bookcase (Amishim)	Fun	20	Serious	High
		Bookcase (Libri di Regina)	Fun	30	Serious	High
Chair (Living Room)	Sit	Wicker	Comfort	20	N/A	Medium
		Country Class	Comfort	20	N/A	Medium
		Citronel	Comfort	20	N/A	Medium
		Sarrbach	Comfort	20	N/A	Medium
Chair (Dining Room)	Sit	Werkbunnst	Comfort	25	N/A	Medium
		Teak	Comfort	25	N/A	Medium
		Empress	Comfort	25	N/A	Medium
		Parisienne	Comfort	25	N/A	Medium
Chair (Office/Deck)	Sit	Office Chair	Comfort	20	N/A	Medium
		Deck Chair	Comfort	20	N/A	Medium
Chair (Recliner)	Nap	Both Recliners	Energy	15	Lazy	High
		Both Recliners	Comfort	20	Lazy	Medium
	Sit	Both Recliners	Comfort	30	Lazy	Medium
Chess	Join	Chess Set	Fun	40	Outgoing	High
			Social	40	N/A	Medium
	Play		Fun	35	Serious	High
Clock (Grandfather)	Wind	N/A	Room	40	Neat	High
Coffee (Espresso Machine)	Drink Espresso	N/A	Energy	115	N/A	Medium
		N/A	Fun	10	N/A	High
		N/A	Bladder	-10	N/A	High
Coffeemaker	Drink Coffee	N/A	Bladder	-5	N/A	High
		N/A	Energy	115	N/A	Medium

OBJECT TYPE	POSSIBLE INTERACTIONS	OBJECT VARIATIONS	ADVERTISED MOTIVE	ADVERTISED VALUE	PERSONALITY TRAIT MODIFIER	REDUCED EFFECTS (OVER DISTANCE)
Computer	Play	Moneywell	Fun	30	Playful	High
		Microscotch	Fun	35	Playful	High
		Brahma	Fun	40	Playful	High
		Marco	Fun	50	Playful	High
	Turn Off	All Computers	Energy	220	Neat	Medium
Dollhouse	Play	N/A	Fun	30	Playful	High
	Watch	N/A	Fun	30	Playful	Medium
		N/A	Social	30	N/A	Medium
Easel	Paint	N/A	Fun	20	N/A	High
Flamingo	Kick	N/A	Mood	15	Grouchy	High
	View	N/A	Fun	10	Playful	High
Flood	Clean	N/A	Room	80	Neat	High
Flowers (Outdoor)	Stomp On	N/A	Mood	10	Grouchy	High
	Water	N/A	Room	20	Neat	Medium
Flowers/Plants (Indoor)	Throw Out	N/A	Room	50	Neat	Medium
	Water	N/A	Room	25	Neat	Medium
Food	Clean	All Meal/ Snack Types	Room	20	Neat	Medium
	Prepare and Eat	BBQ Group Meal	Hunger	90	N/A	Low
		BBQ Single	Hunger	80	N/A	Low
		Candy	Hunger	30	N/A	Low
		Fruitcake (Group Meal)	Hunger	30	N/A	Low
		Fruitcake (Slice)	Hunger	80	N/A	Low
		Light Meal	Hunger	80	N/A	Low
		Pizza Box	Hunger	90	N/A	Low
		Pizza Slice	Hunger	80	N/A	Low
		Regular Group Meal	Hunger	90	N/A	Low
		Regular Single Meal	Hunger	80	N/A	Low
		Snack	Hunger	25	N/A	Low

OBJECT TYPE	POSSIBLE INTERACTIONS	OBJECT VARIATIONS	ADVERTISED MOTIVE	ADVERTISED VALUE	PERSONALITY TRAIT MODIFIER	REDUCED EFFECTS (OVER DISTANCE)
Fountain	Play	N/A	Fun	10	Shy	High
Refrigerator	Have Meal	All Fridges	Hunger	65	N/A	Low
	Have Snack	Llamark	Hunger	20	N/A	Low
		Porcina	Hunger	30	N/A	Low
		Freeze Secret	Hunger	40	N/A	Low
	Have Quick Meal	All Fridges	Hunger	55	N/A	Low
	Serve Meal	All Fridges	Hunger	70	Cooking	Low
		All Fridges	Energy	-10	N/A	Low
Gift (Flowers)	Clean	N/A	Room	30	Neat	Medium
Hot Tub	Get In	N/A	Fun	45	Lazy	High
		N/A	Comfort	50	N/A	High
		N/A	Social	25	Outgoing	Medium
		N/A	Hygiene	5	N/A	Medium
	Join	N/A	Comfort	30	N/A	Low
		N/A	Fun	50	Outgoing	Low
		N/A	Social	50	N/A	Low
		N/A	Hygiene	5	N/A	Medium
Lava Lamp	Turn On	N/A	Room	5	N/A	High
		N/A	Fun	5	N/A	High
Mailbox	Get Mail	N/A	Comfort	10	N/A	High
		N/A	Hunger	10	N/A	High
		N/A	Hygiene	10	N/A	High
		N/A	Room	10	N/A	High
Medicine Cabinet	Brush Teeth	N/A	Hygiene	25	Neat	Medium
Newspaper	Clean Up	N/A	Room	50	Neat	Medium
	Read	N/A	Fun	5	Serious	High
Painting	View	N/A	Fun	5	Serious	High
Phone	Answer	N/A	Fun	50	N/A	Medium
		N/A	Comfort	50	N/A	Medium
		N/A	Social	50	N/A	Medium
Piano	Play	N/A	Fun	40	Strong Creativity	High
	Watch	N/A	Fun	70	N/A	Medium
		N/A	Social	10	N/A	Medium

OBJECT TYPE	POSSIBLE INTERACTIONS	OBJECT VARIATIONS	ADVERTISED MOTIVE	ADVERTISED VALUE	PERSONALITY TRAIT MODIFIER	REDUCED EFFECTS (OVER DISTANCE)
Pinball Machine	Join	N/A	Fun	50	N/A	Medium
		N/A	Social	30	N/A	Medium
	Play	N/A	Fun	40	Playful	High
Play Structure	Join	N/A	Fun	60	Playful	Medium
		N/A	Social	40	N/A	Medium
	Play	N/A	Fun	60	Playful	Medium
Pool Diving Board	Dive In	N/A	Fun	35	Active	High
		N/A	Energy	-10	N/A	High
Pool Table	Join	N/A	Fun	50	Playful	Low
		N/A	Social	40	N/A	Low
	Play	N/A	Fun	45	Playful	High
Sculpture	View	Scylla and Charybdis	Fun	6	Serious	High
		Bust of Athena	Fun	5	Serious	High
		Large Black Slab	Fun	8	Serious	High
		China Vase	Fun	7	Serious	High
Shower	Clean	N/A	Room	20	Neat	High
	Take a Shower	N/A	Hygiene	50	Neat	Medium
Sink	Wash Hands	N/A	Hygiene	10	Neat	High
Sofa/Loveseat	Nap	All Sofas/Loveseats	Energy	40	Lazy	High
		All Sofas/Loveseats	Comfort	5	Lazy	High
	Sit	All Sofas/Loveseats	Comfort	30	Lazy	Medium
		Garden Bench	Comfort	30	Lazy	Medium
Stereo	Dance	Boom Box	Social	40	Outgoing	High
			Fun	50	Active	High
		Zimantz Hi-Fi	Social	50	Outgoing	High
			Fun	60	Active	High
		Strings Theory	Social	60	Outgoing	High
			Fun	70	Active	High
	Join	Boom Box	Social	40	Outgoing	Low

OBJECT TYPE	POSSIBLE INTERACTIONS	OBJECT VARIATIONS	ADVERTISED MOTIVE	ADVERTISED VALUE	PERSONALITY TRAIT MODIFIER	REDUCED EFFECTS (OVER DISTANCE)
Stereo			Fun	40	Outgoing	Low
		Zimantz Hi-Fi	Social	50	Outgoing	Low
			Fun	40	Outgoing	Low
		Strings Theory	Social	60	Outgoing	Low
			Fun	40	Outgoing	Low
	Turn Off	All Stereos	Energy	220	Neat	Medium
	Turn On	Boom Box	Fun	25	Playful	High
		Zimantz Hi-Fi	Fun	25	Playful	High
		Strings Theory	Fun	30	Playful	High
Toilet	Clean	Both Toilets	Room	40	Neat	High
	Flush	Hygeia-O-Matic	Room	30	Neat	High
	Unclog	Both Toilets	Room	50	Neat	High
	Use	Hygeia-O-Matic	Bladder	50	N/A	Low
		Flush Force	Bladder	70	N/A	Low
Tombstone/ Urn	Mourn (first 24 hours)	N/A	Bladder	5	N/A	Low
		N/A	Comfort	50	N/A	Low
		N/A	Energy	5	N/A	Low
		N/A	Fun	50	N/A	Low
		N/A	Hunger	5	N/A	Low
		N/A	Hygiene	50	N/A	Low
		N/A	Social	50	N/A	Low
		N/A	Room	50	N/A	Low
	Mourn (second 48 hours)	N/A	Bladder	0	N/A	Low
		N/A	Comfort	30	N/A	Low
		N/A	Energy	0	N/A	Low
		N/A	Fun	30	N/A	Low
		N/A	Hunger	0	N/A	Low
		N/A	Hygiene	30	N/A	Low
		N/A	Social	30	N/A	Low
		N/A	Room	30	N/A	Low
Toy Box	Play	N/A	Fun	55	Playful	Medium

OBJECT TYPE	POSSIBLE INTERACTIONS	OBJECT VARIATIONS	ADVERTISED MOTIVE	ADVERTISED VALUE	PERSONALITY TRAIT MODIFIER	REDUCED EFFECTS (OVER DISTANCE)
Train Set (Large)	Play	N/A	Fun	40	N/A	Medium
	Watch	N/A	Fun	40	N/A	Low
		N/A	Social	40	N/A	Low
Train Set (Small)	Play	N/A	Fun	45	Playful	Medium
	Watch	N/A	Fun	20	N/A	Medium
		N/A	Social	30	N/A	Medium
Trash Can (Inside)	Empty Trash	N/A	Room	30	Neat	Medium
Trash Compactor	Empty Trash	N/A	Room	30	N/A	High
Trash Pile	Clean	N/A	Room	75	Neat	Medium
Bathtub	Clean	All Tubs	Room	20	Neat	High
	Bathe	Justa	Hygiene	50	Neat	Medium
		Justa	Comfort	20	N/A	Medium
		Sani-Queen	Hygiene	60	Neat	Medium
		Sani-Queen	Comfort	25	N/A	Medium
		Hydrothera	Hygiene	70	Neat	Medium
		Hydrothera	Comfort	30	N/A	Medium
TV	Join	Monochrome	Fun	20	Lazy	High
		Trottco	Fun	30	Lazy	High
		Soma Plasma	Fun	45	Lazy	High
	Turn Off	All TVs	Energy	220	Neat	Medium
	Turn On	Monochrome	Fun	18	Lazy	High
		Trottco	Fun	35	Lazy	High
		Soma Plasma	Fun	49	Lazy	High
	Watch TV	Monochrome	Fun	18	Lazy	High
		Trottco	Fun	28	Lazy	High
		Soma Plasma	Fun	42	Lazy	High
VR Glasses	Play	N/A	Fun	60	Playful	High

CHAPTER 3:
INTERACTING WITH OTHER SIMS

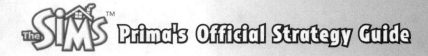

Introduction

Once you get beyond the dark attraction of watching jilted Sims slap their rivals, or obnoxious Sims insulting their friends, you realize that Relationships are very important to your Sims' quality of life, and even to the advancement of their careers. In this chapter, we introduce you to the world of Relationships, covering the possible events that occur when two Sims come together verbally or physically. Our goal here is to lay down the ground rules. We'll offer hands-on tips for building and maintaining Relationships in the "All in the Family" chapter.

Relationship Scores

Icons representing a Sim's friendships, or lack thereof, appear in the screen's lower-right corner when you click on the Relationships icon (just above the Job icon). The scoring system ranges from below 0 (not good) to 100, which is reserved for one or more significant others. A relationship is considered a true friendship if the score climbs above 50. Only these Relationships are considered when the game calculates career advancements. Consult the next chapter, "9 to 5: Climbing the Career Ladder," for more information on promotion requirements.

Fig. 3-1. This Sim Dad is clicking on all cylinders with his wife, but he needs to spend more time with the kids.

Social Interactions

All Sim Relationships develop from Social interactions. If you don't spend quality time with your friends, the Relationships will deteriorate on their own, at a rate of two points per day. Of course, if you interact poorly, the rate accelerates dramatically. In the following sections, we review the myriad communication choices that are available during the game (grouped alphabetically by the active action). At any given time, your choice will vary, depending upon the level of your friendship, and whether or not your Sim is acting like a jerk!

Good Old Conversation

The easiest way to cultivate a new friendship is to talk. Sims communicate with each either using Sim-Speak, a delightful chatter that you actually begin to understand (yes, we have played this game way too much!). Adults and kids have favorite topics within their peer groups. These topics are randomly assigned by the game during the Sim creation process. Additionally, kids and adults have special cross-generational topics that are only used with each other. Active topics are displayed in thought balloons during the game, as shown in figure 3-2.

Fig. 3-2. Pets are a good common ground for conversation between adults and kids.

When a conversation is going well, you see a green plus sign over one or both of the Sims. Conversely, when talk deteriorates into the gutter, you'll see red minus signs. The following tables list positive and negative communications, including each potential outcome and the corresponding effect on Social and Relationship scores. For our purposes, an outcome is positive if it produces an increase in one or both scores. When scores drop or stay the same, it is considered a negative outcome.

Fig. 3-3. When two or more people enter a hot tub, the conversations begin spontaneously.

Positive Communications

INTERACTION	RESPONSE	RELATIONSHIP CHANGE	SOCIAL SCORE CHANGE
Apologize	Accept	10	15
Be Apologized To	Accept	10	15
Brag	Good	5	13
Be Bragged To	Good	5	7
Cheer Up	Good	5	7
Cheer Up	Neutral	0	5
Be Cheered Up	Good	10	10
Be Cheered Up	Neutral	0	5
Compliment	Accept	5	5
Be Complimented	Accept	5	11
Entertain	Laugh	4	7
Be Entertained	Laugh	8	13
Flirt	Good	5	13
Be Flirted With	Good	10	13
Joke	Laugh	5	13
Joke	Giggle	2	7
Listen to Joke	Laugh	7	13
Listen to Joke	Giggle	3	7
Scare	Laugh	5	10
TalkHigh Interest	Topic	3	5
TalkLike	Topic	3	5
Group Talk	N/A	1	8
Tease	Giggle	5	7

Negative Communications

INTERACTION	RESPONSE	RELATIONSHIP CHANGE	SOCIAL SCORE CHANGE
Apologize	Reject	-10	0
Be Apologized To	Reject	-10	0
Brag	Bad	-5	0
Be Bragged To	Bad	-5	0
Cheer Up	Bad	-3	0
Be Cheered Up	Bad	-10	0
Compliment	Reject	-10	0
Be Complimented	Reject	-7	0
Entertain	Boo	-15	0
Be Entertained	Boo	-7	0
Flirt	Refuse	-10	-17
Flirt	Ignore	-5	0
Be Flirted With	Refuse	-10	0
Be Flirted With	Ignore	0	0
Insult	Cry	5	0
Insult	Stoic	0	3
Insult	Angry	-10	7
Be Insulted	Cry	-12	-13
Be Insulted	Stoic	-5	-5
Be Insulted	Angry	-14	-7
Joke	Uninterested	-6	0
Listen to Joke	Uninterested	-7	0
Scare	Angry	-5	0
Be Scared	Angry	-10	0
TalkDislike	Topic	-3	3
TalkHate	Topic	-3	3
Tease	Cry	-4	0
Be Teased	Cry	-13	-7

Physical Contact

When a Relationship moves past the 50-point threshold, you begin to see new options on the Social interaction menu. Instead of just talking, you find new items including Hug, Give Back Rub, Flirt, and Kiss. It all depends upon how your Relationship is progressing and what the other Sim is looking for in the current interaction. The following tables include information on positive and negative physical events.

Positive Physical Events

INTERACTION	RESPONSE	RELATIONSHIP CHANGE	SOCIAL SCORE CHANGE
Give Back Rub	Good	5	7
Receive Back Rub	Good	9	13
Dance	Accept	8	13
Be Danced With	Accept	10	13
Give Gift	Accept	5	7
Receive Gift	Accept	10	13
Hug	Good	7	15
Hug	Tentative	2	7
Be Hugged	Good	8	15
Be Hugged	Tentative	4	7
Kiss	Passion	12	20
Kiss	Polite	5	10
Be Kissed	Passion	12	20
Be Kissed	Polite	5	10
Tickle	Accept	5	13
Be Tickled	Accept	8	13

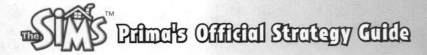

Negative Physical Events

INTERACTION	RESPONSE	RELATIONSHIP CHANGE	SOCIAL SCORE CHANGE
Attack	Win Fight	-5	10
Attack	Lose Fight	-10	-20
Give Back Rub	Bad	-7	0
Receive Back Rub	Bad	-10	0
Dance	Refuse	-5	0
Be Danced With	Refuse	-5	0
Give Gift	Stomp	-15	0
Receive Gift	Stomp	-5	0
Hug	Refuse	-10	0
Be Hugged	Refuse	-10	0
Kiss	Deny	-15	5
Be Kissed	Deny	-10	0
Slap	Cry	0	3
Slap	Slap Back	-10	-7
Be Slapped	Cry	-20	-17
Be Slapped	Slap Back	-15	7
Tickle	Refuse	-5	0
Be Tickled	Refuse	-8	0

CHAPTER 4:
9 TO 5—CLIMBING THE
CAREER LADDER

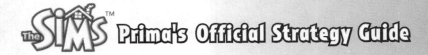

Introduction

When you first start playing *The Sims*, it's easy to get lost in the element. There's so much to explore and experience, and with more than enough money to furnish your house and buy a few toys, you can just hang out and live the good Sim-life. But, reality sets in sooner than you would like, and you must find a job. In this chapter we show you how to select a career, nurture the Skills necessary to earn the first few promotions, and finally, stockpile enough friends (it's called networking) to make the big bucks and zoom to the top of your field. For easy reference, we include comprehensive career tables that contain everything you need to know about the 10 Sim careers, including advancement requirements for all 10 pay levels.

Your First Job

Every Sim house receives a daily copy of the *Sim City Times* that includes a single job posting. You can take the first job you see, or buy a computer and view three jobs a day. There is no rush—you have enough money to get by for several days.

Fig. 4-1. Today's job posting is for a test driver.

You can enjoy the free use of a computer by buying it, checking the want ads, and then returning it the same day for a full refund. Keep this up until you find the job you want. Then, later when you have more disposable cash, you can buy—and keep—a computer.

A Military job is usually available on the computer. This is an excellent first career, with a starting salary of §250. Furthermore, it remains the highest paying of the 10 careers through the first three advances. A Law Enforcement position is a close second.

Fig. 4-2. This two-commando family takes home §325 each as members of the Elite Forces (Level 2—Military Career).

If you would rather take your time and sort through all 10 job tracks, the following table will help you choose a career that is suited to your Sim's personality traits.

Career Choices

CAREER TRACK	NECESSARY SKILLS	RELATED PERSONALITY TRAITS
Business	Logic, Charisma	Outgoing
Entertainment	Charisma, Creativity	Outgoing, Playful
Law Enforcement	Logic, Body	Active
Life of Crime	Creativity, Charisma	Playful, Outgoing
Medicine	Logic, Body	Active
Military	Repair, Body	Active
Politics	Charisma, Logic	Outgoing
Pro Athlete	Body, Charisma	Active, Outgoing
Science	Logic, Creativity	Playful
Xtreme	Creativity, Body/Charisma (tie)	Playful, Active, Outgoing

Developing Your Skills

After you decide on a career, focus on developing the appropriate Skills needed for advancement. It is important to remember that Sims do not study on their own. You need to direct your Sim to one of the activities listed in the Skill Enhancement table below.

On the control panel, click on the Job icon to display your Sim's current Skill bars (see figure 4-3). A white line designates the minimum level of Skill needed for the next promotion. Other factors contribute to earning a promotion, but without the Skill requirement, you have absolutely no chance for advancement to the next level.

Fig. 4-3. This Sim needs to boost his Body Skill one more notch, so he is scheduled for a session on the exercise machine right after lunch.

Skill Enhancement

SKILL	METHOD OF ENHANCEMENT	NOTES
Cooking	Bookshelf (Study Cooking)	Any type of bookshelf will suffice.
Mechanical	Bookshelf (Study Mechanical)	Any type of bookshelf will suffice.
Body	Exercise Machine (Work Out)	Exercise machine increases Skill four times faster than the pool. Active Sims improve their Skill at a higher rate.
	Pool (Swim)	See above.
Charisma	Mirrors or Medicine Cabinet (Practice Speech)	Outgoing Sims acquire Skill more quickly.
	Easel (Paint)	Playful Sims acquire Skill more quickly.
	Piano (Play)	Playful Sims acquire Skill more quickly.
Logic	Chessboard (Play)	Playing with another Sim generates Social points.

Fig. 4-4. A session on the exercise bench nets a Body point for this Sim.

Sim Career Tracks

The following tables include the salaries, hours, car pool vehicles, and job level requirements for each level of the 10 Sim career tracks. The Daily Motive Decay value shows which Motives deteriorate while the Sim is on the job.

Requirements for Level 1 Positions

CAREER TRACK	POSITION	PAY	HOURS	CAR POOL VEHICLE	COOKING	REPAIR	CHARISMA	BODY	LOGIC	CREATIVITY	FAMILY/ FRIENDS	DAILY MOTIVE DECAY						
												HUNGER	COMFORT	HYGIENE	BLADDER	ENERGY	FUN	SOCIAL
Business	Mail Room	§120	9 a.m. –3 p.m.	Junker	0	0	0	0	0	0	0	0	0	0	0	-30	0	0
Entertainment	Waiter Waitress	§100	9 a.m. –3 p.m.	Junker	0	0	0	0	0	0	0	0	0	0	0	-30	0	0
Law Enforcement	Security Guard	§240	12 a.m. –6 a.m.	Squad Car	0	0	0	0	0	0	0	0	0	0	0	-30	0	0
Life of Crime	Pickpocket	§140	9 a.m. –3 p.m.	Junker	0	0	0	0	0	0	0	0	0	0	0	-30	0	0
Medicine	Medical Technician	§200	9 a.m. –3 p.m.	Junker	0	0	0	0	0	0	0	0	0	0	0	-30	0	0
Military	Recruit	§250	6 a.m. –12 p.m.	Military Jeep	0	0	0	0	0	0	0	0	0	-15	0	-30	0	0
Politics	Campaign Work	§220	9 a.m. –6 p.m.	Junker	0	0	0	0	0	0	0	0	0	0	0	-30	0	0
Pro Athlete	Team Mascot	§110	12 p.m. –6 p.m.	Junker	0	0	0	0	0	0	0	0	0	-5	0	-35	0	0
Science	Test Subject	§155	9 a.m. –3 p.m.	Junker	0	0	0	0	0	0	0	0	0	0	0	-30	0	0
Xtreme	Daredevil	§175	9 a.m. –3 p.m.	Junker	0	0	0	0	0	0	0	0	0	0	0	-30	0	0

Requirements for Level 2 Positions

CAREER TRACK	POSITION	PAY	HOURS	CAR POOL VEHICLE	COOKING	REPAIR	CHARISMA	BODY	LOGIC	CREATIVITY	FAMILY/ FRIENDS	DAILY MOTIVE DECAY						
												HUNGER	COMFORT	HYGIENE	BLADDER	ENERGY	FUN	SOCIAL
Business	Executive Assistant	§180	9 a.m. –4 p.m	Junker	0	0	0	0	0	0	0	0	0	0	0	-34	-2	0
Entertainment	Extra	§150	9 a.m. –3 p.m.	Junker	0	0	0	0	0	0	0	0	0	0	0	-34	-2	0
Law Enforcement	Cadet	§320	9 a.m. –3 p.m.	Squad Car	0	0	0	0	0	0	0	0	0	0	0	-34	-2	0
Life of Crime	Bagman	§200	11 p.m. –7 a.m.	Junker	0	0	0	0	0	0	0	0	0	0	0	-34	-2	0
Medicine	Paramedic	§275	11 p.m. –5 a.m.	Junker	0	0	0	0	0	0	0	0	0	0	0	-34	-2	0
Military	Elite Forces	§325	7 a.m. –1 p.m.	Military Jeep	0	0	0	0	0	0	0	0	0	-15	0	-34	-2	0
Politics	Intern	§300	9 a.m. –3 p.m.	Junker	0	0	0	0	0	0	0	0	0	0	0	-34	-2	0
Pro Athlete	Minor Leaguer	§170	9 a.m. –3 p.m.	Junker	0	0	0	0	0	0	0	0	0	-10	0	-40	-2	0
Science	Lab Assistant	§230	11 p.m. –5 a.m.	Junker	0	0	0	0	0	0	0	0	0	0	0	-34	-2	0
Xtreme	Bungee Jump Instructor	§250	9 a.m. –3 p.m.	Junker	0	0	0	0	0	0	0	0	0	0	0	-34	-2	0

Requirements for Level 3 Positions

Career Track	Position	Pay	Hours	Car Pool Vehicle	Cooking	Repair	Charisma	Body	Logic	Creativity	Family/Friends	Daily Motive Decay						
												Hunger	Comfort	Hygiene	Bladder	Energy	Fun	Social
Business	Field Sales Rep	§250	9 a.m.–4 p.m.	Junker	0	2	0	0	0	0	0	-3	0	-5	0	-38	-4	0
Entertainment	Bit Player	§200	9 a.m.–3 p.m.	Junker	0	0	2	0	0	0	0	-3	0	-5	0	-38	-4	0
Law Enforcement	Patrol Officer	§380	5 p.m.–1 a.m.	Squad Car	0	0	0	2	0	0	0	-3	0	-5	0	-38	-4	0
Life of Crime	Bookie	§275	12 p.m.–7 p.m.	Standard Car	0	0	0	2	0	0	0	-3	0	-5	0	-38	-4	0
Medicine	Nurse	§340	9 a.m.–3 p.m.	Standard Car	0	2	0	0	0	0	0	-3	0	-5	0	-38	-4	0
Military	Drill Instructor	§250	8 a.m.–2 p.m.	Military Jeep	0	0	0	2	0	0	0	-3	0	-20	0	-38	-4	0
Politics	Lobbyist	§360	9 a.m.–3 p.m.	Standard Car	0	0	2	0	0	0	0	-3	0	-5	0	-38	-4	0
Pro Athlete	Rookie	§230	9 a.m.–3 p.m.	Junker	0	0	0	2	0	0	0	-3	0	-15	0	-45	-2	0
Science	Field Researcher	§320	9 a.m.–3 p.m.	Standard Car	0	0	0	0	2	0	0	-3	0	-5	0	-38	-4	0
Xtreme	Whitewater Guide	§325	9 a.m.–3 p.m.	SUV	0	0	0	2	0	0	1	-3	0	-10	0	-45	-4	0

Requirements for Level 4 Positions

Career Track	Position	Pay	Hours	Car Pool Vehicle	Cooking	Repair	Charisma	Body	Logic	Creativity	Family/Friends	Daily Motive Decay						
												Hunger	Comfort	Hygiene	Bladder	Energy	Fun	Social
Business	Junior Executive	§320	9 a.m.–4 p.m.	Standard Car	0	2	2	0	0	0	1	-7	0	-10	0	-42	-7	0
Entertainment	Stunt Double	§275	9 a.m.–4 p.m.	Standard Car	0	0	2	2	0	0	2	-7	0	-10	0	-42	-7	0
Law Enforcement	Desk Sergeant	§440	9 a.m.–3 p.m.	Squad Car	0	2	0	2	0	0	1	-7	0	-10	0	-42	-7	0
Life of Crime	Con Artist	§350	9 a.m.–3 p.m.	Standard Car	0	0	1	2	0	1	2	-7	0	-10	0	-42	-7	0
Medicine	Intern	§410	9 a.m.–6 p.m.	Standard Car	0	2	0	2	0	0	2	-7	0	-10	0	-42	-7	0
Military	Junior Officer	§450	9 a.m.–3 p.m.	Military Jeep	0	1	2	2	0	0	0	-7	0	-20	0	-42	-8	0
Politics	Campaign Manager	§430	9 a.m.–6 p.m.	Standard Car	0	0	2	0	1	0	2	-7	0	-10	0	-42	-7	0
Pro Athlete	Starter	§300	9 a.m.–3 p.m.	Standard Car	0	0	0	5	0	0	1	-7	0	-20	0	-50	-2	0
Science	Science Teacher	§375	9 a.m.–4 p.m.	Standard Car	0	0	1	0	3	0	1	-7	0	-10	0	-40	-7	0
Xtreme	Xtreme Circuit Pro	§400	9 a.m.–3 p.m.	SUV	0	1	0	4	0	0	2	-7	0	-20	0	-50	-2	0

Requirements for Level 5 Positions

CAREER TRACK	POSITION	PAY	HOURS	CAR POOL VEHICLE	COOKING	REPAIR	CHARISMA	BODY	LOGIC	CREATIVITY	FAMILY/ FRIENDS	DAILY MOTIVE DECAY						
												HUNGER	COMFORT	HYGIENE	BLADDER	ENERGY	FUN	SOCIAL
Business	Executive	§400	9 a.m.–4 p.m.	Standard Car	0	2	2	0	2	0	3	-10	0	-15	0	-46	-10	0
Entertainment	B-Movie Star	§375	10 a.m.–5 p.m.	Standard Car	0	0	3	3	0	1	4	-10	0	-15	0	-46	-10	0
Law Enforcement	Vice Squad	§490	10 p.m.–4 a.m.	Squad Car	0	3	0	4	0	0	2	-10	0	-15	0	-46	-10	0
Life of Crime	Getaway Driver	§425	5 p.m.–1 a.m.	Standard Car	0	2	1	2	0	2	3	-10	0	-10	0	-46	-10	0
Medicine	Resident	§480	9 p.m.–4 a.m.	Standard Car	0	3	0	2	2	0	3	-10	0	-15	0	-46	-10	0
Military	Counter-Intelligence	§500	9 a.m.–3 p.m.	Military Jeep	1	1	2	4	0	0	0	-10	0	-25	0	-46	-12	0
Politics	City Council Member	§485	9 a.m.–3 p.m.	Town Car	0	0	3	1	1	0	4	-10	0	-15	0	-46	-8	0
Pro Athlete	All-Star	§385	9 a.m.–3 p.m.	SUV	0	1	1	6	0	0	3	-10	0	-25	0	-55	-3	0
Science	Project Leader	§450	9 a.m.–5 p.m.	Standard Car	0	0	2	0	4	1	3	-10	0	-12	0	-43	-8	0
Xtreme	Bush Pilot	§475	9 a.m.–3 p.m.	SUV	1	2	0	4	1	0	3	-10	0	-15	0	-46	-5	-10

Requirements for Level 6 Positions

CAREER TRACK	POSITION	PAY	HOURS	CAR POOL VEHICLE	COOKING	REPAIR	CHARISMA	BODY	LOGIC	CREATIVITY	FAMILY/ FRIENDS	DAILY MOTIVE DECAY						
												HUNGER	COMFORT	HYGIENE	BLADDER	ENERGY	FUN	SOCIAL
Business	Senior Manager	§520	9 a.m.–4 p.m.	Standard Car	0	2	3	0	3	2	6	-14	0	-20	0	-50	-13	0
Entertainment	Supporting Player	§500	10 a.m.–6 p.m.	Limo	0	1	4	4	0	2	6	-14	0	-20	0	-50	-13	0
Law Enforcement	Detective	§540	9 a.m.–3 p.m.	Squad Car	1	3	1	5	1	0	4	-14	0	-20	0	-50	-13	0
Life of Crime	Bank Robber	§530	3 p.m.–11 p.m.	Town Car	0	3	2	3	1	2	4	-14	0	-15	0	-50	-13	-5
Medicine	GP	§550	10 a.m.–6 p.m.	Town Car	0	3	1	3	4	0	4	-14	0	-20	0	-50	-13	0
Military	Flight Officer	§550	9 a.m.–3 p.m.	Military Jeep	1	2	4	4	1	0	1	-14	0	-28	0	-50	-15	0
Politics	State Assembly-person	§540	9 a.m.–4 p.m.	Town Car	0	0	4	2	1	1	6	-14	0	-20	0	-50	-12	-3
Pro Athlete	MVP	§510	9 a.m.–3 p.m.	SUV	0	2	2	7	0	0	5	-14	0	-30	0	-60	-4	0
Science	Inventor	§540	10 a.m.–7 p.m.	Town Car	0	2	2	0	4	3	4	-14	0	-15	0	-45	-9	-8
Xtreme	Mountain Climber	§550	9 a.m.–3 p.m.	SUV	1	4	0	6	1	0	4	-14	0	-30	0	-60	0	0

Requirements for Level 7 Positions

CAREER TRACK	POSITION	PAY	HOURS	CAR POOL VEHICLE	COOKING	REPAIR	CHARISMA	BODY	LOGIC	CREATIVITY	FAMILY/ FRIENDS	DAILY MOTIVE DECAY						
												HUNGER	COMFORT	HYGIENE	BLADDER	ENERGY	FUN	SOCIAL
Business	Vice President	§660	9 a.m. –5 p.m.	Town Car	0	2	4	2	4	2	8	-18	0	-25	0	-54	-16	0
Entertainment	TV Star	§650	10 a.m. –6 p.m.	Limo	0	1	6	5	0	3	8	-18	0	-25	0	-54	-16	0
Law Enforcement	Lieutenant	§590	9 a.m. –3 p.m.	Limo	1	3	2	5	3	1	6	-18	0	-25	0	-54	-16	0
Life of Crime	Cat Burglar	§640	9 p.m. –3 a.m.	Town Car	1	3	2	5	2	3	6	-18	0	-20	0	-54	-16	0
Medicine	Specialist	§625	10 p.m. –4 a.m.	Town Car	0	4	2	4	4	1	5	-18	0	-25	0	-54	-16	0
Military	Senior Officer	§580	9 a.m. –3 p.m.	Military Jeep	1	3	4	5	3	0	3	-18	0	-31	0	-55	-20	0
Politics	Congress- person	§600	9 a.m. –3 p.m.	Town Car	0	0	4	3	3	2	9	-18	0	-25	0	-54	-18	-7
Pro Athlete	Superstar	§680	9 a.m. –4 p.m.	SUV	1	2	3	8	0	0	7	-18	0	-35	0	-65	-5	0
Science	Scholar	§640	10 a.m. –3 p.m.	Town Car	0	4	2	0	6	4	5	-18	0	-20	0	-48	-10	-10
Xtreme	Photo- journalist	§650	9 a.m. –3 p.m.	SUV	1	5	2	6	1	3	5	-18	0	-25	0	-54	-16	0

Requirements for Level 8 Positions

CAREER TRACK	POSITION	PAY	HOURS	CAR POOL VEHICLE	COOKING	REPAIR	CHARISMA	BODY	LOGIC	CREATIVITY	FAMILY/ FRIENDS	DAILY MOTIVE DECAY						
												HUNGER	COMFORT	HYGIENE	BLADDER	ENERGY	FUN	SOCIAL
Business	President	§800	9 a.m. –5 p.m.	Town Car	0	2	5	2	6	3	10	-22	0	-30	0	-58	-19	0
Entertainment	Feature Star	§900	5 p.m. –1 a.m.	Limo	0	2	7	6	0	4	10	-22	0	-30	0	-58	-19	0
Law Enforcement	SWAT Team Leader	§625	9 a.m. –3 p.m.	Limo	1	4	3	6	5	1	8	-22	0	-30	0	-58	-19	0
Life of Crime	Counterfeiter	§760	9 p.m. –3 a.m.	Town Car	1	5	2	5	3	5	8	-22	0	-25	0	-58	-19	-15
Medicine	Surgeon	§700	10 p.m. –4 a.m.	Town Car	0	4	3	5	6	2	7	-22	0	-30	0	-58	-19	0
Military	Commander	§600	9 a.m. –3 p.m.	Military Jeep	1	6	5	5	5	0	5	-22	0	-33	0	-60	-25	0
Politics	Judge	§650	9 a.m. –3 p.m.	Town Car	0	0	5	4	4	3	11	-22	0	-30	0	-58	-22	-11
Pro Athlete	Assistant Coach	§850	9 a.m. –2 p.m.	SUV	2	2	4	9	0	1	9	-22	0	-40	0	-70	-6	0
Science	Top Secret Researcher	§740	10 a.m. –3 p.m.	Town Car	1	6	4	0	7	4	7	-22	0	-25	0	-52	-12	-13
Xtreme	Treasure Hunter	§725	10 a.m. –5 p.m.	SUV	1	6	3	7	3	4	7	-22	0	-34	0	-60	-15	-5

Requirements for Level 9 Positions

CAREER TRACK	POSITION	PAY	HOURS	CAR POOL VEHICLE	COOKING	REPAIR	CHARISMA	BODY	LOGIC	CREATIVITY	FAMILY/ FRIENDS	DAILY MOTIVE DECAY						
												HUNGER	COMFORT	HYGIENE	BLADDER	ENERGY	FUN	SOCIAL
Business	CEO	§950	9 a.m.–4 p.m.	Limo	0	2	6	2	7	5	12	-26	0	-35	0	-62	-22	0
Entertainment	Broadway Star	§1100	10 a.m.–5 p.m.	Limo	0	2	8	7	0	7	12	-26	0	-35	0	-62	-22	0
Law Enforcement	Police Chief	§650	9 a.m.–5 p.m.	Limo	1	4	4	7	7	3	10	-26	0	-35	0	-62	-22	0
Life of Crime	Smuggler	§900	9 a.m.–3 p.m.	Town Car	1	5	5	6	3	6	10	-26	0	-30	0	-62	-22	-20
Medicine	Medical Researcher	§775	9 p.m.–4 a.m.	Limo	0	5	4	6	8	3	9	-26	0	-35	0	-62	-22	0
Military	Astronaut	§625	9 a.m.–3 p.m.	Limo	1	9	5	8	6	0	6	-26	0	-35	0	-65	-30	0
Politics	Senator	§700	9 a.m.–6 p.m.	Limo	0	0	6	5	6	4	14	-26	0	-35	0	-62	-26	-15
Pro Athlete	Coach	§1,000	9 a.m.–3 p.m.	SUV	3	2	6	10	0	2	11	-26	0	-45	0	-75	-8	0
Science	Theorist	§870	10 a.m.–2 p.m.	Town Car	1	7	4	0	9	7	8	-26	0	-30	0	-56	-16	-16
Xtreme	Grand Prix Driver	§825	10 a.m.–4 p.m.	Bentley	1	6	5	7	5	7	9	-26	0	-35	0	-62	-5	-10

Requirements for Level 10 Positions

CAREER TRACK	POSITION	PAY	HOURS	CAR POOL VEHICLE	COOKING	REPAIR	CHARISMA	BODY	LOGIC	CREATIVITY	FAMILY/ FRIENDS	DAILY MOTIVE DECAY						
												HUNGER	COMFORT	HYGIENE	BLADDER	ENERGY	FUN	SOCIAL
Business	Business Tycoon	§1,200	9 a.m.–3 p.m.	Limo	0	2	8	2	9	6	14	-30	0	-40	0	-66	-25	0
Entertainment	Superstar	§1,400	10 a.m.–3 p.m.	Limo	0	2	10	8	0	10	14	-30	0	-40	0	-66	-25	0
Law Enforcement	Captain Hero	§700	10 a.m.–4 p.m.	Limo	1	4	6	7	10	5	12	-20	-80	-45	-25	-60	0	0
Life of Crime	Criminal Mastermind	§1,100	6 p.m.–12 a.m.	Limo	2	5	7	6	4	8	12	-30	0	-35	0	-66	-25	-25
Medicine	Chief of Staff	§850	9 p.m.–4 a.m.	Hospital Limo	0	6	6	7	9	4	11	-30	0	-40	0	-66	-25	0
Military	General	§650	9 a.m.–3 p.m.	Staff Sedan	1	10	7	10	9	0	8	-30	0	-40	0	-70	-35	0
Politics	Mayor	§750	9 a.m.–3 p.m	Limo	0	0	9	5	7	5	17	-30	0	-40	0	-66	-30	-20
Pro Athlete	Hall of Famer	§1,300	9 a.m.–3 p.m.	Limo	4	2	9	10	0	3	13	-30	0	-50	0	-80	-10	0
Science	Mad Scientist	§1,000	10 a.m.–2 p.m.	Limo	2	8	5	0	10	10	10	-30	0	-35	0	-60	-20	-20
Xtreme	International	§925	11 a.m.–5 p.m.	Bentley	2	6	8	8	6	9	11	-30	0	-30	0	-70	-20	-15

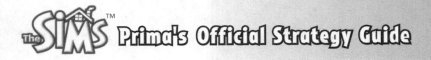
The Daily Grind

A working Sim needs to follow a schedule that is conducive to good job performance. Review the following tips as you devise a work schedule for your household.

Get Plenty of Sleep

Sims need to awake refreshed in order to arrive at work in a good mood. Send your Sims to bed early, and make sure there are no distractions (stereos, TVs, computers, etc.) that might interrupt their beauty sleep.

Fig. 4-5. Make sure your Sims get to bed early enough to restore maximum Energy before the alarm rings.

Set Your Alarm Clock

When set, the clock wakes your Sims two hours before the car pool arrives (one alarm clock takes care of the entire house). This is plenty of time to take care of Hunger, Bladder, and Hygiene Motive bars. If you still have time, improve your Sim's mood with a little non-strenuous fun like watching TV, or use the extra time to improve a Skill.

Fig. 4-6. That last set on the exercise bench paid off!

CAUTION

If two or more Sims in the house have jobs, the alarm clock rings for the earliest riser. Unfortunately, this wakes everyone else, regardless of when they have to be ready for the car pool. If you send the other Sims back to bed, you'll need to wake them manually, because the alarm clock only rings once each day.

Eat a Hearty Breakfast

When you're angling for a promotion, you need to arrive at work with all cylinders firing. When the alarm rings, send the designated house chef (the Sim with the highest Cooking Skill) to the kitchen to "Prepare a Meal." By the time your Sim is finished emptying his Bladder and completing necessary Hygiene, breakfast will be on the counter. There should be plenty of time to complete the meal and head to work with a full Hunger bar.

TIP

Make sure that your Sim is on the first floor and relatively close to the car pool within 15 minutes of departure to be sure he or she catches his or her ride. If you meet this deadline, your Sim will change clothes on the fly and sprint to the curb.

Make Friends and Influence Your Boss

Advancing through the first three levels does not carry a friendship requirement; however this ramps up very quickly. It helps to have a stay-at-home mate to concentrate on making friends. Remember that the career friendship requirement is for your household, not your Sim. So, if your mate or children have friends, they count toward your promotions, too.

Fig. 4-7. This Sim is just about out of Energy, but his Social score is maxed out and he's just made two new friends.

Take an Occasional Day Off to Recharge

If you find that your Sim is unable to have enough Fun or Social events to maintain a positive mood, skip a day of work and indulge. See a friend or two, work on Skills, or have some Fun. Just don't miss two days in a row or your Sim will be automatically fired!

Major Decisions

As you work your way up the career ladder, you encounter "major decisions" that involve various degrees of risk. They are winner-take-all, loser-gets-nada events that force you to gamble with your salary, integrity, or even your job. The following sections include a sample "major decision" for each career.

Business

Major decision: "Stock Option"

Player is given the choice of accepting a portfolio of company stock instead of salary for that pay period. The stock could double or tank. As a result, the player receives twice his salary or nothing at all for the pay period.

Entertainment

Major decision: "The Remake"

Your agent calls with an offer: Sim Studios wants you for the lead in a remake of *Citizen Kane*. Accepting will either send your Charisma sky high when the film succeeds wildly…or send it crashing if the turkey flops.

Law Enforcement

Major decision: "The Bribe"

A mobster you're investigating offers a huge bribe to drop the case. The charges won't stick without your testimony and you *could* suddenly "lose the evidence" and quietly pocket a nice nest egg…or get busted by Internal Affairs and have to start over on a new career track.

Life of Crime

Major decision: "The Perfect Crime"

You've just been handed a hot tip that an informant claims will be an easy knockover with loads of cash for the taking. Either the tip is gold, or it's a police sting. An arrest means your family is left at home alone while you're sent off to cool your heels in Sim City Prison for a while. If you succeed, your Charisma and Creativity Skills are enhanced.

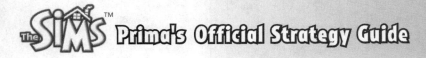

Medicine

Major Decision: "Malpractice"

A former patient has slapped you with a massive malpractice suit. You can settle immediately by offering a payment equal to 50 percent of the cash in your household account. Or, take the bum to court. Lose, and all your furniture and household goods are repossessed. Win, and you receive a settlement equal to 100 percent of the cash in your household account.

Military

Major decision: "Gung Ho"

The general needs volunteers for a highly dangerous mission. You can refuse without penalty. If you accept, and succeed on the mission, you are decorated and immediately promoted to the next level. Failure means a demotion, soldier— you're broken down to the previous level.

Politics

Major decision: "Scandal"

An attractive young member of your team also happens to be heir to a fortune. He or she will finance your career advancement if you agree to "private consultations." You can refuse, with no change in status. Otherwise, there are two possible outcomes. You might get away with it and immediately advance *two* levels. If you're caught, you'll lose your friends when the scandal breaks in the media, and you'll be tossed from the career track to seek another.

Pro Athlete

Major Decision: "The Supermatch"

A one-on-one, pay-per-view contest pitting you against your greatest local rival is offered. If you win, it's worth double your paycheck. If you lose, the indignity comes complete with an injury costing you a reduction in your Body Skill along with a drop in Charisma. The player can always refuse at no penalty.

Science

Major decision: "The Experiment"

A science research firm is willing to pay you a fat bonus for conducting a complex experiment. However, the work must be conducted at your home, using rats as test subjects. Success means you collect the fee, with a bonus increase in your Logic Skill level. A failed experiment results in a dozen rats escaping into your home. That means a major bill from both your exterminator and your electrician (the rats have chewed through power cords.) Financial damage could be reduced if the Player's Repair Skills are strong.

Xtreme

Major decision: "Deep Freeze"

An arctic expedition is holding a spot open for you. It's a risky enterprise, so you may refuse. However, for a person in your particular line of work, that refusal will lower your Charisma. If you join the team, and they reach their goal, you will be rewarded with a considerable rise in Charisma. If the mission goes awry, your Sim is "lost on an iceberg" for a period of game time.

CHAPTER 5:
BUILDING A HOUSE

Introduction

Anyone who has ever built a home knows that the best laid plans of architects can sometimes turn into a house of horrors when the walls start going up. The same holds true in *The Sims*, where you have enough power to build a magnificent dream house or your worst residential nightmare. Limited only by your bank account, you can build a conservative dwelling that is functional above all else, or you can drop a family of eight in the middle of a meadow with only a bathroom and a refrigerator. It's all possible in *The Sims*, but rest assured that your family will deliver a quick—and sometimes scathing—critique when the clock starts ticking on their simulated lives.

In this chapter, we take you through the house design process from terrain preparation to landscaping. For demonstration purposes, we will use just about every building option available. Obviously, you would need a pile of Simoleans to do this in the game. However, we also cover important design considerations that enable you to maximize your Room score, regardless of your budget. In this chapter, we limit our discussion to the available options in Build Mode only. For detailed descriptions of more than 150 *Sims* objects, see the next chapter.

Of course, our suggestions are just the beginning. Sims thrive on the individuality of their creator, and if you want to build dungeons, sprawling compounds, or one-room huts, you have our support and encouragement. Remember, a bad house is no match for the bulldozer—your next house is only a click away!

Don't try to build your dream house at the beginning of the game. It's easier to tear down your original house and start over after you've fattened up your bank account.

Design Considerations

Before we introduce you to the various options available in Build Mode, here is a checklist for your basic floor plan. Invariably, your unique family of Sims will make their needs known to you as the game progresses. However, if you follow these house design basics, you should get your family off to a positive start with a minimum of emotional outbursts.

* **Don't worry about having room to expand. Build your first house to match the number of Sims in your family.**
* **Keep the bathroom centrally located. A door on either side allows quick access for emergencies.**
* **If you start with three Sims or more, build one or more half-bathrooms (toilet and sink only) to ease the crunch.**
* **Place the house close to the street, so you don't have to do the hundred yard dash to meet your car pool.**
* **Allow enough open wall for your kitchen countertops and appliances.**
* **Make your kitchen large enough to accommodate a small table and chairs.**
* **If you don't want a separate den or family room, make one of the bedrooms large enough to handle a computer desk and chair.**

Terrain Tools

In most locations, you can build a roomy house on a flat piece of land without having to level the terrain. However, if you want to build a house near the water or at the edge of a hill, you'll need to smooth the sloping tiles before building a wall, as displayed in figure 5-1.

Fig. 5-1. You can't place a wall section until you smooth the slope.

The Terrain Tool (shovel icon) can be a little tricky to master. On level ground, you can place the shovel at any intersection of horizontal and vertical grid lines, and then click to level, lower, or raise the tile. However, sometimes, due to extreme depth or elevation (usually at the edge of a gully or alongside water), you can't access this intersecting point. When this occurs, you receive a message telling you that the tile cannot be modified (figure 5-2).

TIP

The grid lines become noticeably darker when a previously elevated or lowered tile becomes level.

Fig. 5-2. You cannot level a tile at the water's edge.

In most cases, there is no need to edit the terrain, unless you want to add a sunken hot tub or drop an outdoor play set into a pit. Remember that you must level the ground in the pit before you can place an object (see figure 5-3).

Fig. 5-3. You cannot place the play set until the tiles in the pit are level.

Wall and Fence Tools

There are several tools here, but your first step is to "frame" your house. Simply place the cursor at any tile intersection. Then click, hold, and drag to place your wall (figure 5-4). When you release the mouse button, the wood framing will change to the type of wall you selected on the Control Panel (see page 52 for descriptions of wall types).

Fig. 5-4. Drag and release to place a wall.

Although you must start a wall at an intersection, you are not limited to square walls. Simply drag the cursor at an angle to create an interesting corner (figure 5-5). However, don't make the angled walls too long. You cannot place doors, windows, or objects on these walls. Also, you cannot connect an angled wall to an existing straight wall inside your house.

Wall Tool

Wall Types

NAME	COST (PER SECTION)	DESCRIPTION
White Picket Fence	§10	Outdoor fencing
Privacy Fence	§35	8-foot outdoor fence
Monticello Balustrade	§45	Railings for balconies and stairs
Wrought Iron Balustrade	§45	Railings for balconies and stairs
Tumbleweed Wooden Column	§70	Support columns for second stories or patio covers
Wall Tool	§70	Basic unfinished wall
The Zorba Ionic Column	§80	Classic, white Graeco-Roman column
Chester Brick Column	§100	All brick, squared off column

Fig. 5-5. Angled corners help you transform a boring box into a custom home.

Door and Window Tools

Door Tool

Sims are very active. They seek the best path for their current task, and they think nothing of going out one exterior door and back in through another, if it's the best route. The least expensive Walnut Door (figure 5-6) is only §100, but because it is solid, your Room score does not benefit from outside light. If at all possible, invest in one of the windowed doors, and ideally, pick the multi-paned Monticello Door for maximum light.

Fig. 5-6. The Walnut Door gives your Sims privacy, but it doesn't allow outside light to improve your Room score.

Door Types

NAME	COST	NOTES
Walnut Door	§100	Solid door without windows
Maple Door Frame	§150	Wooden door frame for rooms that do not require total privacy
Federal Lattice Window Door	§200	Glass panes in the upper half of door
Windsor Door	§300	Designer leaded glass door
Monticello Door	§400	7 rows of 3 panes, topped with a 6-pane half circle, allow maximum light to flow into your home

Window Tool

Let the sun shine in to pump up your Room score. Sims love light, so install plenty of windows from the start. Simply click on the selected window and place it on any right-angle wall (remember, you cannot place doors, windows, or objects on a diagonal wall). Window style is strictly personal—all windows exert the same positive effect on the Room score.

TIP

For aesthetic value, match your windows to your door style, such as the Monticello Door with Monticello Windows, as pictured in figure 5-7.

Fig. 5-7. Monticello Doors and Windows provide maximum light.

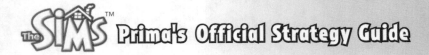
Window Types

NAME	COST	DESCRIPTION
Single-Pane Fixed Window	§50	This economy window still lets in the sun.
Single-Hung Window	§55	This looks good over the kitchen sink.
Privacy Window	§60	Tired of the neighborhood peeping Toms? This window is positioned higher on the wall.
Plate Glass Window	§65	This one's strictly glass from floor to ceiling.
El Sol Window	§80	This round ornamental window is a nice change from square and rectangular styles.
Monticello Window	§110	Use as a bedroom window to complement the Monticello door.
Windsor Window	§120	This ornamental natural wood window adds turn-of-the-century character to your home.
Monticello Window Full-Length	§200	This dramatic window looks beautiful on either side of a Monticello door.

Floor Tool

Unless you like grass in your living room, use the Floor Tool to lay some flooring inside your house. *The Sims* also includes outdoor flooring that works well in patios, backyard barbecue areas, or as pathways to a pool or play area. One tile covers a single grid, and you can quickly finish an entire room with a single shift-click. The price range for floor coverings is §10–§20, and you have a selection of 29 different styles/colors.

> **TIP**
>
> *When you lay flooring inside a room with angled walls, half of the floor tiles appear on the other side of the wall, in another room or outside the house (see figure 5-8). To remove these outside tiles, place any floor type over the tiles, hold down the [Ctrl] key, and then click to delete them. The flooring on the other side of the wall remains undisturbed.*

Fig. 5-8. After you finish the inside flooring, go back and delete the external tiles.

> **NOTE**
>
> *You can use any type of flooring inside or outside.*

Flooring Types

- **Carpeting (7)**
- **Cement (1)**
- **Ceramic Tile-Small Tiles (3)**
- **Checkerboard Linoleum (1)**
- **Clay Paver Tiles (1)**
- **Colored Pavement (1)**
- **Granite (2)**
- **Gravel (1)**
- **Hardwood Plank (1)**
- **Inlaid Hardwood (1)**
- **Italian Tile (1)**
- **Poured Concrete (1)**
- **Shale (1)**
- **Striped Pavement (2, Both Directions)**
- **Tatami Mats (2)**
- **Terracotta Tile (1)**
- **Wood Parquet (2)**

Wallpaper Tool

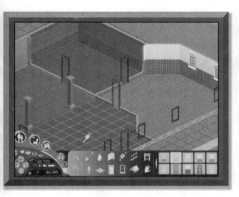

Fig. 5-9. Use the Wallpaper Tool to create a different mood in every room.

There are 30 different indoor/outdoor wall coverings in *The Sims,* and just as with floor coverings, you are limited only by your budget and sense of style. Prices range from §4 for basic wallpaper to §14 for granite block. If you change your mind after putting up the wallpaper, you can rip it down and get your money back by holding down the [Ctrl] key and clicking on the ugly panel.

Wallpaper Types

- **Adobe (1)**
- **Aluminum Siding (1)**
- **Brick (2)**
- **Granite (1)**
- **Interior Wall Treatments (6 Fabric and Paint Combinations)**
- **Japanese Paper/Screens (4)**
- **Paint (4)**
- **Plaster (1)**
- **Stucco (1)**
- **Tudor (1)**
- **Wainscoting (1)**
- **Wallpaper (4)**
- **Wood Clapboard (1)**
- **Wood Paneling (1)**
- **Wood Shingles (1)**

Stair Tool

You may not plan to build a second story immediately, but it's still a good idea to place your staircase before you start filling your house with objects. Choose from four staircases, two at §900 and two at §1,200. But, no matter how much you spend, they still get your Sims up and down the same way.

Style is considerably less important than function. You don't want to interrupt the traffic flow inside your house, especially to critical rooms such as the bathroom and kitchen. For this reason, staircases work well against a wall, where they are out of the way, or between two large, open rooms, such as the kitchen and family room (figure 5-10).

Fig. 5-10. Both of these placements keep the staircases out of the main traffic patterns.

If you don't have the money to finish the second story, just place the staircase and forget about it. The Sims won't go upstairs until you add a second story. After the staircase is positioned, the process for building a second story is exactly the same as building the first floor. The only obvious difference is that the buildable wall space extends out one square beyond the walls on the first floor. This allows you to squeeze a little extra space for a larger room or balcony.

Roof Tool

Although it is much easier to play The Sims using the Walls Cutaway or Walls Down options on the Control Panel, you will want to step back and enjoy your masterpiece in all of its crowning glory. The Roof Tool allows you to select a Shallow, Medium, or Steep Pitch for your roof, and choose from a selection of four roof patterns.

Fig. 5-11. Our house has a Steep Pitch with dark roof tiles.

Water Tools

Now that you have walls, floors, and doors, it's time to add a pool. Of course, this isn't a necessity, but your Sims love to swim, and it's an easy way to add important Body points. After placing your pool, don't forget to add a diving board so your Sims can get in, and a ladder so they can climb out. As you build your pool, the Water Tool places light-colored cement squares as decking. You can go back and cover these tiles with the outdoor surface of your choice, as displayed in figure 5-12. You can also add fencing around your deck to give your pool a more finished look.

Fig. 5-12. With the pool and decking in place, you have room to add an outdoor barbecue and beverage cart.

Fireplace Tool

Fig. 5-13. It looks innocent enough, but a roaring fire can turn nearby objects or Sims into a deadly inferno.

When placed safely out of the way of flammable objects, a fireplace adds a major boost to the Room score. However, it can be a dangerous fire hazard if Sims wander too close, so give it a wide berth when a fire is roaring.

Plant Tool

Now, it's time to put the finishing touches on the exterior of your house. Using the Plant Tool, you can select from 14 different plants, priced from §5 for Wildflowers to §300 for an Apple Tree. The following types of vegetation are included:

Plant Types

• **Flowers (4)**

• **Bushes (1)**

• **Hedges (2)**

• **Shrubs (2)**

• **Trees (5)**

Let your green thumb go wild, but don't forget that only trees and shrubs will thrive without regular watering. If you want colorful flowers, you'll probably need to hire a Gardener.

Fig. 5-14. This colorful landscaping will require the services of a Gardener, or a Sim with a lot of time to kill.

Special Editing Tools

In addition to the building tools described above, there are two other options on the Build Mode Control Panel. The curved arrows pictured at the bottom corner of figure 5-15 allow you to undo or repeat your last action(s). This is a quick way to delete unwanted items.

Fig. 5-15. Click Undo Last to reverse your most recent actions.

If the undo button is unavailable, you can click on the Hand Tool, select any object, and then press the Delete key to sell it back. For directions on how to delete walls, wall coverings, and floor coverings, see the appropriate sections in this chapter.

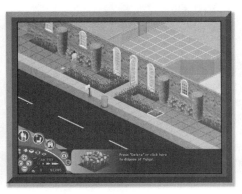

Fig. 5-16. Select an item with the Hand Tool, then press Delete to make it go away.

CHAPTER 6:
MATERIAL SIMS

Introduction

This chapter covers the eight categories of objects available in Buy Mode: Seating, Surfaces, Decorative, Electronics, Appliances, Plumbing, Lighting, and Miscellaneous. Every object is listed with its purchase price, related Motives, and Efficiency ratings. You can shop 'til you drop, but it's more important to buy smart than to buy often. Our comprehensive Buying Guide is just ahead, but first let's study some important factors that impact your spending habits.

Buying for Needs, Instead of Needing to Buy

If you select a ready-made house for your new Sim family, you acquire walls, floors, and a roof, but little else. The house is empty, with nary a toilet, bed, or refrigerator in sight. Depending upon how much you spent on the house, you'll have a few thousand Simoleans to use in Buy Mode, where you can purchase more than 150 objects. Most objects affect your Sims' environment in positive ways. However, not every object is a necessity. In fact, if you are a recovering shopping channel addict, this is not a good time to fall off your wallet. Make your first purchases with The Sims' Motives (or Needs) in mind. You can review your Sims' current Needs state by clicking on the Mood icon. We provide detailed descriptions in the Motives chapter, but for now, here is a basic shopping list that will help you get your Sims' Need bars out of the red zone during the early stages of a game.

In most instances, an expensive item has a greater impact on the related Need bar than an economy model. For example, a §300 cot gives your Sim a place to crash, but a §3,000 Mission Bed provides more Comfort and lets your Sim get by on less sleep. As an added bonus, the top-of-the-line bed also adds to the overall Room score.

Fig. 6-1. Despite logging only five hours of sleep, Bella is feeling pretty good, thanks to her §3000 Mission bed.

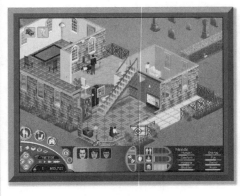

Fig. 6-2. A big-screen TV is fun for your Sims, but also for the neighbors, who will often hang out, and boost your Social score.

NEED	ITEM	EXPLANATION
Hunger	Refrigerator, Food Processor, Stove	A refrigerator alone will sustain life, but you will greatly improve the quality of Sim meals by using a food processor and stove. However, there is a risk of fire if your Sim doesn't have at least two Cooking Skill points.
Comfort	Bed, Chairs	Sims will sleep anywhere when they are tired, but a bed is highly recommended for sleeping, and you'll need chairs (for eating and working at the computer), and a couch for napping. A bathtub provides a little extra comfort for your Sims, but it isn't critical, provided you have a shower.
Hygiene	Sink, Shower	Dirty Sims spend a lot of time waving their arms in the air to disperse their body odor. Not a pretty sight. Fortunately, a sink and shower go a long way toward improving their state of mind (not to mention the smell).
Bladder	Toilet	When you gotta go, you gotta go. Sims prefer using a toilet, but if one is not available, they will relieve themselves on the floor. This not only causes great shame and embarrassment, but someone in your family will have to clean up the mess. It's also very bad for your Hygiene levels.
Energy	Bed	If you don't want to spawn a family of insomniacs, buy a sufficient number of beds for your Sims. A shot of coffee or espresso provides a temporary Energy boost, but it is definitely not a long-term solution.
Fun	TV	The boob tube is the easiest and cheapest way to give your Sims a break from their daily grinds. You can add other, more exciting, items later, but this is your best choice early on.
Social	Telephone	Ignore this for a short time while you focus on setting up your house. However, don't force your Sims into a solitary lifestyle. Other Sims may walk by the house, but you'll have better results after buying a telephone, so that you can invite people over and gain Social points when they arrive.
Room	Windows, Lamps, Decorations, Landscaping	Sims like plenty of light, from windows during the day and artificial lighting at night. Table Lamps are the cheapest, but they can only be placed on raised surfaces. As your game progresses, you can add decorations and landscaping to boost the Room score.

Sims Can Be Hard to Please

Given a fat bank account, it would seem that you can always cheer up your Sims with a few expensive purchases. Not exactly. While you are spending your hard-earned Simoleans, the Sims are busy comparing everything that you buy to everything they already own. If you fail to keep your Sims in the manner to which they are accustomed, their responses to your new objects may be indifferent or even downright negative. Every time you make a purchase, the game uses an assessment formula to calculate your Sim's response. The logic goes like this:

Fig. 6-3. Compared to the §2,100 "Snails With Icicles in Nose," this §45 clown picture doesn't quite stack up.

Your Diminishing Net Worth

When times are tough, you may need to raise cash by selling objects in your house. With rare exception, you will never match your initial investment, thanks to instant depreciation, and as time goes on, your belongings continue to lose value until they reach their depreciation limits. The following table lists every object in *The Sims* (alphabetically), including purchase price and depreciated values.

- Calculates the average value of everything in your house (including outdoor items).

- Subtracts 10 percent of the new object's value for each existing copy of the same item. Don't expect your family members to jump for joy if you add a hot tub to every room in the house.

- Compares the value of the new object with all existing objects in your house. If the new purchase is worth 20 percent or more above the average value of current items, the Sim exhibits a positive response by clapping.

- If the new object is within 20 percent (above or below) of the current average value of all items in your household, the Sim gives you an uninspired shrug.

- If the new object is less than 20 percent below the average value, your Sim waves it off and you'll see a red X through the object.

Although depreciation reduces the value of your furnishings over time, there is a buyer's remorse period when you can return the item for full value (if it has been less than 24 hours since you purchased it). So, if you have second thoughts about that new hot tub, simply select the item and hit the Delete key to get your money back.

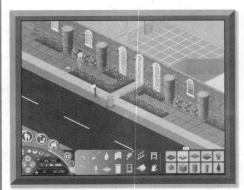

Fig. 6-4. This Pyrotorre Gas Range is §1,000 new, but after depreciation it's worth only §790.

Object Depreciation

NAME	PURCHASE PRICE	INITIAL DEPRECIATION	DAILY DEPRECIATION	DEPRECIATION LIMIT
Alarm: Burglar	§250	§62	§2	§50
Alarm: Smoke	§50	§12	§0	§10
Aquarium	§200	§30	§2	§80
Bar	§800	§120	§8	§320
Barbecue	§350	§70	§4	§105
Basketball Hoop (Cheap Eaze)	§650	§98	§6	§260
Bed: Double	§450	§68	§4	§180
Bed: Double (Mission)	§3,000	§450	§30	§1,200
Bed: Double (Napoleon)	§1,000	§150	§10	§400
Bed: Single (Spartan)	§300	§45	§3	§120
Bed: Single (Tyke Nyte)	§450	§68	§4	§180
Bench: Garden	§250	§38	§2	§100
Bookshelf: Amishim	§500	§75	§5	§200
Bookshelf: Libri di Regina	§900	§135	§9	§360
Bookshelf: Pine	§250	§38	§2	§100
Chair: Deck (Survivall)	§150	§22	§2	§60
Chair: Dining (Empress)	§600	§90	§6	§240
Chair: Dining (Parisienne)	§1,200	§180	§12	§480
Chair: Dining (Teak)	§200	§30	§2	§80
Chair: Dining (Werkbunnst)	§80	§12	§1	§32
Chair: Living Room (Citronel)	§450	§68	§4	§180
Chair: Living Room (Country Class)	§250	§38	§2	§100
Chair: Living Room (Sarrbach)	§500	§75	§5	§200
Chair: Living Room (Wicker)	§80	§12	§1	§32
Chair: Office	§100	§15	§1	§40

NAME	PURCHASE PRICE	INITIAL DEPRECIATION	DAILY DEPRECIATION	DEPRECIATION LIMIT
Chair: Recliner (Back Slack)	§250	§38	§2	§100
Chair: Recliner (Von Braun)	§850	§128	§8	§340
Chess Set	§500	§75	§5	§200
Clock: Alarm	§30	§4	§0	§12
Clock: Grandfather	§3,500	§525	§35	§1,400
Coffee: Espresso Machine	§450	§90	§4	§135
Coffeemaker	§85	§17	§1	§26
Computer (Brahma 2000)	§2,800	§700	§28	§560
Computer (Marco)	§6,500	§1,625	§65	§1,300
Computer (Microscotch)	§1,800	§450	§18	§360
Computer (Moneywell)	§999	§250	§10	§200
Counter: Bath (Count Blanc)	§400	§60	§4	§160
Counter: Kitchen (Barcelona: In)	§800	§120	§8	§320
Counter: Kitchen (Barcelona: Out)	§800	§120	§8	§320
Counter: Kitchen (NuMica)	§150	§22	§2	§60
Counter: Kitchen (Tiled)	§250	§38	§2	§100
Desk (Cupertino)	§220	§33	§2	§88
Desk (Mesquite)	§80	§12	§1	§32
Desk (Redmond)	§800	§120	§8	§320
Dishwasher (Dish Duster)	§550	§110	§6	§165
Dishwasher (Fuzzy Logic)	§950	§190	§10	§285
Dollhouse	§180	§27	§2	§72
Dresser (Antique Armoire)	§1,200	§180	§12	§480
Dresser (Kinderstuff)	§300	§45	§3	§120

NAME	PURCHASE PRICE	INITIAL DEPRECIATION	DAILY DEPRECIATION	DEPRECIATION LIMIT
Dresser (Oak Armoire)	§550	§82	§6	§220
Dresser (Pinegulcher)	§250	§38	§2	§100
Easel	§250	§38	§2	§100
Exercise Machine	§700	§105	§7	§280
Flamingo	§12	§2	§0	§5
Food Processor	§220	§44	§2	§66
Fountain	§700	§105	§7	§280
Fridge (Freeze Secret)	§2,500	§500	§25	§750
Fridge (Llamark)	§600	§120	§6	§180
Fridge (Porcina)	§1,200	§240	§12	§360
Hot Tub	§6,500	§1,300	§65	§1,950
Lamp: Floor (Halogen)	§50	§8	§0	§20
Lamp: Floor (Lumpen)	§100	§15	§1	§40
Lamp: Floor (Torchosteronne)	§350	§52	§4	§140
Lamp: Garden	§50	§7	§1	§20
Lamp: Love n' Haight Lava	§80	§12	§1	§32
Lamp: Table (Antique)	§300	§45	§3	§120
Lamp: Table (Bottle)	§25	§4	§0	§10
Lamp: Table (Ceramiche)	§85	§13	§1	§34
Lamp: Table (Elite)	§180	§27	§2	§72
Medicine Cabinet	§125	§19	§1	§50
Microwave	§250	§50	§2	§75
Mirror: Floor	§150	§22	§2	§60
Mirror: Wall	§100	§15	§1	§40
Phone: Tabletop	§50	§12	§0	§10
Phone: Wall	§75	§19	§1	§15
Piano	§3,500	§525	§35	§1,400
Pinball Machine	§1,800	§450	§18	§360
Plant: Big (Cactus)	§150	§22	§2	§60
Plant: Big (Jade)	§160	§24	§2	§64
Plant: Big (Rubber)	§120	§18	§1	§48

NAME	PURCHASE PRICE	INITIAL DEPRECIATION	DAILY DEPRECIATION	DEPRECIATION LIMIT
Plant: Small (Geranium)	§45	§7	§0	§18
Plant: Small (Spider)	§35	§5	§0	§14
Plant: Small (Violets)	§30	§4	§0	§12
Play Structure	§1,200	§180	§12	§480
Pool Table	§4,200	§630	§42	§1,680
Shower	§650	§130	§6	§195
Sink: Bathroom Pedestal	§400	§80	§4	§120
Sink: Kitchen (Double)	§500	§100	§5	§150
Sink: Kitchen (Single)	§250	§50	§2	§75
Sofa (Blue Pinstripe)	§400	§60	§4	§160
Sofa (Contempto)	§200	§30	§2	§80
Sofa (Country)	§450	§68	§4	§180
Sofa (Deiter)	§1,100	§165	§11	§440
Sofa (Dolce)	§1,450	§218	§14	§580
Sofa (Recycled)	§180	§27	§2	§72
Sofa (SimSafari)	§220	§33	§2	§88
Sofa: Loveseat (Blue Pinstripe)	§360	§54	§4	§144
Sofa: Loveseat (Contempto)	§150	§22	§2	§60
Sofa: Loveseat (Country)	§340	§51	§3	§136
Sofa: Loveseat (Indoor-Outdoor)	§160	§24	§2	§64
Sofa: Loveseat (Luxuriare)	§875	§131	§9	§350
Stereo (Strings)	§2,550	§638	§26	§510
Stereo (Zimantz)	§650	§162	§6	§130
Stereo: Boom Box	§100	§25	§1	§20
Stove (Dialectric)	§400	§80	§4	§120
Stove (Pyrotorre)	§1,000	§200	§10	§300
Table: Dining (Colonial)	§200	§30	§2	§80
Table: Dining (Mesa)	§450	§68	§4	§180

NAME	PURCHASE PRICE	INITIAL DEPRECIATION	DAILY DEPRECIATION	DEPRECIATION LIMIT
Table: Dining (NuMica)	§95	§14	§1	§38
Table: Dining (Parisienne)	§1,200	§180	§12	§480
Table: End (Anywhere)	§120	§18	§1	§48
Table: End (Imperious)	§135	§20	§1	§54
Table: End (KinderStuff)	§75	§11	§1	§30
Table: End (Mission)	§250	§38	§2	§100
Table: End (Pinegulcher)	§40	§6	§0	§16
Table: End (Sumpto)	§300	§45	§3	§120
Table: End (Wicker)	§55	§8	§1	§22
Table: Outdoor (Backwoods)	§200	§30	§2	§80
Toaster Oven	§100	§20	§1	§30
Toilet (Flush Force)	§1,200	§240	§12	§360
Toilet (Hygeia-O-Matic)	§300	§60	§3	§90
Tombstone/Urn	§5	§1	§0	§2
Toy Box	§50	§8	§0	§20
Train Set: Large	§955	§239	§10	§191
Train Set: Small	§80	§20	§1	§16
Trash Compactor	§375	§75	§4	§112
Tub (Hydrothera)	§3,200	§640	§32	§960
Tub (Justa)	§800	§160	§8	§240
Tub (Sani-Queen)	§1,500	§300	§15	§450
TV (Monochrome)	§85	§21	§1	§17
TV (Soma)	§3,500	§875	§35	§700
TV (Trottco)	§500	§125	§5	§100
VR Glasses	§2,300	§575	§23	§460

The Sims Buying Guide

The following sections represent the eight item categories that appear when you click the Buy Mode button on the control panel. We've added a few subcategories to make it easier to find a specific object. The Efficiency Value (1–10) indicates how well the item satisfies each Motive. You get what you pay for in *The Sims*, so an §80 chair doesn't quite stack up to an §850 recliner when it comes to boosting your Comfort level, and it cannot restore Energy.

Seating

Chairs

There are three types of chairs in *The Sims*: movable, stationary, and reclining. Any chair will function at a desk or table for eating and using objects. If your budget is tight, you can also use cheaper chairs for watching TV or reading, but their Comfort ratings are very low. You can use high-ticket dining room chairs at the computer, but that is probably overkill. You are better off placing them in the dining room where you receive greater benefit from their enhanced Room ratings.

Stationary chairs are cushier and nicely upholstered (depending on your taste, of course), and they usually provide more comfort. Finally, the reclining chairs are top of the line, giving you increased comfort and the added benefit of being able to catch a few Zs in the reclining position.

Chair placement is critical, especially around tables. A Sim will not move a chair sideways, only forward and backward. So, position the chair properly or the Sim will not be able to use the table (or what is on it). Also, be careful not to trap a Sim in a corner when a chair is pulled out. For example, if a child is playing with a train set in the corner of the room, and another Sim pulls out a chair to use the computer, the child would be trapped in the corner until the computer user is finished.

Werkbunnst All-Purpose Chair

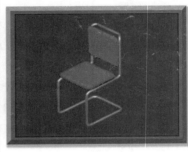

Type: Movable

Cost: §80

Motive: Comfort (2)

Posture Plus Office Chair

Type: Movable

Cost: §100

Motive: Comfort (3)

Deck Chair by Survivall

Type: Movable

Cost: §150

Motive: Comfort (3)

Touch of Teak Dinette Chair

Type: Movable

Cost: §200

Motive: Comfort (3)

Empress Dining Room Chair

Type: Movable

Cost: §600

Motives: Comfort (4), Room (2)

Parisienne Dining Chair

Type: Movable

Cost: §1,200

Motives: Comfort (6), Room (3)

Sioux City Wicker Chair

Type: Stationary

Cost: §80

Motive: Comfort (2)

Country Class Armchair

Type: Stationary

Cost: §250

Motive: Comfort (4)

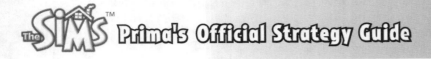

"Citronel" from Chiclettina Inc.

Type: Stationary

Cost: §450

Motive: Comfort (6)

"The Sarrbach" by Werkbunnst

Type: Stationary

Cost: §500

Motive: Comfort (6)

"Back Slack" Recliner

Type: Recliner

Cost: §250

Motives: Comfort (6),
Energy (3)

"Von Braun" Recliner

Type: Recliner

Cost: §850

Motives: Comfort (9),
Energy (3)

Couches

Sitting down is fine for reading, eating, or working, but for serious vegging, your Sims need a good couch. When selecting a couch, function is more important than quality. If you are looking for a place to take naps, pay more attention to the Energy rating than the Comfort or Room ratings. A multipurpose couch should have good Energy and Comfort ratings. However, if you are furnishing your party area, select one that looks good, thereby enhancing your Room rating. Stay away from the cheapest couches (under §200). For a few extra dollars, a medium-priced couch will make your Sims a lot happier. When you're flush with Simoleans, don't forget to dress up your garden with the outdoor bench. You can't sleep on it, but it looks great.

Contempto Loveseat

Cost: §150

Motives: Comfort (3),
Energy (4)

Indoor-Outdoor Loveseat

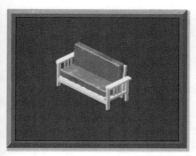

Cost: §160

Motives: Comfort (3), Energy (4)

SimSafari Sofa

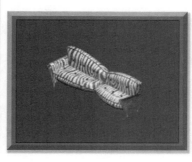

Cost: §220

Motives: Comfort (3), Energy (5)

Recycled Couch

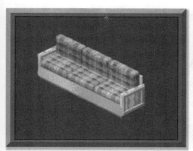

Cost: §180

Motives: Comfort (2), Energy (5)

Parque Fresco del Aire Bench

Cost: §250

Motive: Comfort (2)

Contempto Couch

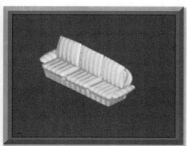

Cost: §200

Motives: Comfort (3), Energy (5)

Country Class Loveseat

Cost: §340

Motives: Comfort (5), Energy (4)

Pinstripe Loveseat from Zecutime

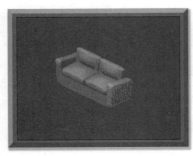

Cost: §360

Motives: Comfort (5),
Energy (4)

Luxuriare Loveseat

Cost: §875

Motives: Comfort (8),
Energy (4), Room (2)

Pinstripe Sofa from Zecutime

Cost: §400

Motives: Comfort (5),
Energy (5)

"The Deiter" by Werkbunnst

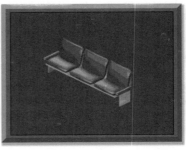

Cost: §1,100

Motives: Comfort (8),
Energy (5), Room (3)

Country Class Sofa

Cost: §450

Motives: Comfort (5),
Energy (5)

Dolce Tutti Frutti Sofa

Cost: §1,450

Motives: Comfort (9),
Energy (5), Room (3)

Beds

Getting enough sleep can be one of the most frustrating goals in *The Sims*, especially if there is a new baby in the house, or your car pool arrives at some ungodly hour of the morning. In the early stages of a game, it is not important to spend a bundle of money on a designer bed. However, an upgrade later on is well worth the money, because a top-of-the-line bed recharges your Energy bar faster.

Spartan Special

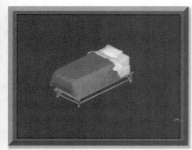

Cost: §300

Motives: Comfort (6), Energy (7)

Cheap Eazzzzze Double Sleeper

Cost: §450

Motives: Comfort (7), Energy (8)

Tyke Nyte Bed

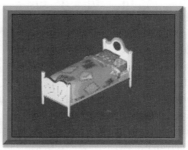

Cost: §450

Motives: Comfort (7), Energy (7)

Napoleon Sleigh Bed

Cost: §1,000

Motives: Comfort (8), Energy (9)

Modern Mission Bed

Cost: §3,000

Motives: Comfort (9), Energy (10), Room (3)

Surfaces

Sims will eat or read standing up if they have to, but they won't be particularly happy about it. Sitting at a table while eating a meal bolsters a Sim's Comfort. Since your Sims have to eat to satisfy Hunger, they might as well improve Comfort, too. Many objects require elevated surfaces, so allow enough room for nightstands (alarm clock, lamps), tables (computer), and countertops (microwave, coffeemaker, etc.), when you design the interior of your house. Also, your Sims cannot prepare food on a table, so provide ample countertop space in the kitchen, or you may find them wandering into the bathroom to chop veggies on the counter (hair in the soup—yummy!).

Countertops

NuMica Kitchen Counter

Cost: §150

Motive: None

Tiled Counter

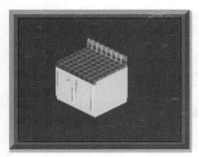

Cost: §250

Motive: None

Count Blanc Bathroom Counter

Cost: §400

Motive: None

"Barcelona" Outcurve Counter

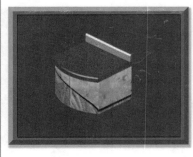

Cost: §800

Motive: Room (2)

"Barcelona" Incurve Counter

Cost: §800

Motive: Room (2)

End Tables

Pinegulcher End Table

Cost: §40

Motive: None

Wicker Breeze End Table

Cost: §55

Motive: None

"Anywhere" End Table

Cost: §120

Motive: None

Imperious Island End Table

Cost: §135

Motive: None

Modern Mission End Table

Cost: §250

Motive: Room (1)

Sumpto End Table

Cost: §300

Motive: Room (1)

KinderStuff Nightstand

Cost: §75

Motive: None

Desks/Tables

Mesquite Desk/Table

Cost: §80

Motive: None

NuMica Folding Card Table

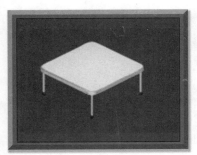

Cost: §95

Motive: None

"Colonial Legacy" Dining Table

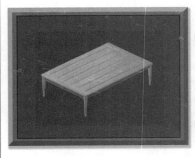

Cost: §200

Motive: None

Backwoods Table by Survivall

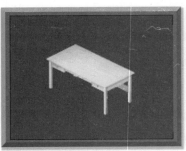

Cost: §200

Motive: None

London "Cupertino" Collection Desk/Table

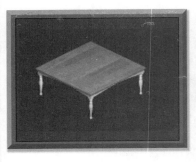

Cost: §220

Motive: None

London "Mesa" Dining Design

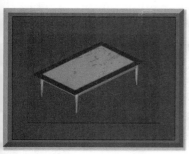

Cost: §450

Motive: Room (2)

The "Redmond" Desk/Table

Cost: §800

Motive: Room (2)

Parisienne Dining Table

Cost: §1,200

Motive: Room (3)

Decorative

After the essential furnishings are in place, you can improve your Room score by adding decorative objects. Some items, such as the grandfather clock and aquarium, require regular maintenance, but most decorative items exist solely for your Sims' viewing pleasure. You might even get lucky and buy a painting or sculpture that increases in value. In addition to enhancing the Room score, the aquarium and fountain have Fun value.

Pink Flamingo

Cost: §12

Motive: Room (2)

African Violet

Cost: §30

Motive: Room (1)

Spider Plant

Cost: §35

Motive: Room (1)

Watercolor by J.M.E.

Cost: §75

Motive: Room (1)

"Roxana" Geranium

Cost: §45

Motive: Room (1)

Rubber Tree Plant

Cost: §120

Motive: Room (2)

"Tragic Clown" Painting

Cost: §45

Motive: Room (1)

Echinopsis maximus Cactus

Cost: §150

Motive: Room (2)

Jade Plant

Cost: §160

Motive: Room (2)

"Delusion de Grandeur"

Cost: §360

Motive: Room (2)

Poseidon's Adventure Aquarium

Cost: §200

Motive: Fun (1), Room (2)

"Fountain of Tranquility"

Cost: §700

Motives: Fun (1), Room (2)

"Bi-Polar" by Conner I.N.

Cost: §240

Motive: Room (2)

Landscape #12,001 by Manny Kopees

Cost: §750

Motive: Room (3)

Bust of Athena by Klassick Repro. Inc.

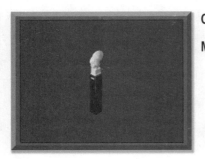

Cost: §875

Motive: Room (3)

"Scylla and Charybdis"

Cost: §1,450

Motive: Room (4)

Snails With Icicles in Nose

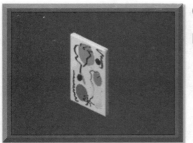

Cost: §2,140

Motive: Room (5)

Portrait Grid by Payne A. Pitcher

Cost: §3,200

Motive: Room (8)

Grandfather Clock

Cost: §3,500

Motive: Room (7)

Blue China Vase

Cost: §4,260

Motive: Room (7)

"Still Life, Drapery and Crumbs"

Cost: §7,600

Motive: Room (9)

"Large Black Slab" by ChiChi Smith

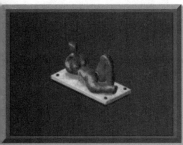

Cost: §12,648

Motive: Room (10)

Electronics

This game offers a veritable potpourri of high-tech gadgetry, ranging from potentially lifesaving items such as smoke detectors to nonessential purchases such as pinball games or virtual reality headsets. Beyond the critical electronics items—smoke detectors, telephone for receiving calls or calling services and friends, TV for cheap fun, and computer for finding a job—you should focus on items with group activity potential, especially if you like socializing and throwing parties.

TIP

Electronic items can break down on a regular basis, so it is a good idea to bone up on Mechanical Skills. Until you have a qualified fix-it Sim in the house, you'll be shelling out §50 an hour for a repairman.

FireBrand Smoke Detector

Cost: §50

Motive: None

Notes: Each detector covers one room. At the very least, place a detector in any room that has a stove or fireplace.

SimSafety IV Burglar Alarm

Cost: §250

Motive: None

Notes: An alarm unit covers one room, but an outside alarm covers an area within five tiles of the house. The police are called immediately when the alarm goes off.

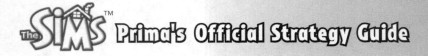

SCTC BR-8 Standard Telephone

Cost: §50

Motive: None

Notes: This phone needs a surface, so it's less accessible. Best location is in the kitchen; stick with wall phones in the rest of the house.

SCTC Cordless Wall Phone

Cost: §75

Motive: None

Notes: Place these phones wherever your Sims spend a lot of time.

Urchineer Train Set by Rip Co.

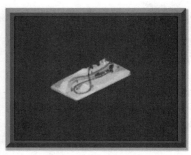

Cost: §80

Motive: Fun (2)

Notes: Group activity; can only be used by kids.

Televisions

Buying a TV is the easiest way to put a little fun into your Sims' lives, and it is a group activity. You can maximize the effect by matching the program category with your Sim's personality, as noted in the following table.

PERSONALITY	FAVORITE TV SHOW
Active	Action
Grouchy (low nice)	Horror
Outgoing	Romance
Playful	Cartoon

Your TV will eventually break down, especially if you have a family of couch potatoes. Do not attempt to repair the TV unless your Sim has at least one Mechanical Skill point (three is even better). If your Sim doesn't have the proper training, poking around inside the TV will result in electrocution.

Monochrome TV

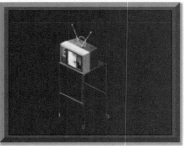

Cost: §85

Motive: Fun (2)

Notes: Strictly for tight budgets, but it gives your Sims a little mindless fun.

Trottco 27" Color Television B94U

Cost: §500

Motive: Fun (4)

Notes: A lazy Sim's favorite activity is watching TV.

Soma Plasma TV

Cost: §3,500

Motive: Fun (6), Room (2)

Notes: It's expensive, but it provides instant entertainment for a full house.

Stereos

Dancing to the music is a great group activity, especially for Sims with effervescent personalities (although it is perfectly acceptable to dance alone). When a Sim dances with a houseguest, it increases both their Fun and Social ratings. You can personalize *The Sims* by placing your own MP3 files in the Music/Stations directory.

"Down Wit Dat" Boom Box

Cost: §100

Motive: Fun (2)

Notes: An inexpensive way to start a party in your front yard.

Zimantz Component Hi-Fi Stereo

Cost: §650

Motive: Fun (3)

Notes: Perfect for your big party room.

Strings Theory Stereo

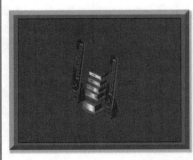

Cost: §2,550

Motives: Fun (5), Room (3)

Notes: The ultimate party machine, this is the only stereo that enhances your Room score.

Computers

A computer is a Sim's best tool for finding a job. The computer has three job postings every day, making it three times as productive as the newspaper employment ads. Aside from career search, the computer provides entertainment for the entire family, and it helps the kids keep their grades up (better chance of cash rewards from the grandparents). Playful and lazy Sims love the computer. However, if only serious Sims occupy your house, you can grab a newspaper and let the age of technology pass you by.

Moneywell Computer

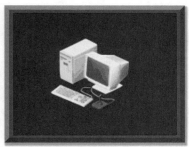

Cost: §999

Motive: Fun (3), Study

Notes: All you need is a basic computer for job searching.

Microscotch Covetta Q628-1500JA

Cost: §1,800

Motive: Fun (5), Study

Notes: More power translates into better gaming.

The Brahma 2000

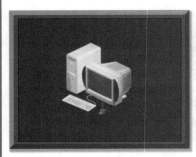

Cost: §2,800

Motive: Fun (7), Study

Notes: More than twice the fun of a basic computer.

Meet Marco

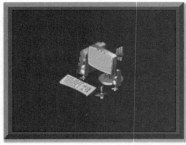

Cost: §6,500

Motive: Fun (9), Study

Notes: For Sim power users—the family will fight for playing time on this beast.

OCD Systems SimRailRoad Town

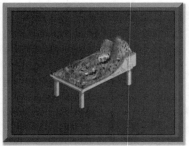

Cost: §955

Motive: Fun (4), Room (3)

Notes: You need a large area for this train table, but it is an excellent group activity and it gives a serious boost to your Room score.

"See Me, Feel Me" Pinball Machine

Cost: §1,800

Motive: Fun (5)

Notes: Build a big family room and add a pinball machine to keep your guests occupied for hours.

SSRI Virtual Reality Set

Cost: §2,300

Motive: Fun (7)

Notes: Playful Sims have been known to don VR glasses on their way to the bathroom (even with full bladders). For grins, wait until a Sim puts on the glasses, then immediately issue another command. The Sim head on the control panel will wear the glasses for the duration of your game.

Appliances

With the exception of the dishwasher and trash compactor, the Sim appliances are all devoted to the creation of food or java. At a bare minimum, you need refrigeration. However, if you want your Sims to eat like royalty, train at least one family member in the gentle art of cooking and provide that Sim with the latest in culinary tools.

Mr. Regular-Joe Coffee

Cost: §85

Motive: Bladder (-1), Energy (1)

Notes: Only adults can partake of the coffee rush. The effects are temporary, but sometimes it's the only way to get rolling.

Gagmia Simore Espresso Machine

Cost: §450

Motive: Bladder (-2), Energy (2), Fun (1)

Notes: If you want a morning jolt, espresso is the way to go. You'll fill your bladder twice as fast as with regular coffee, but it is a small price to pay for more energy and a splash of fun.

Brand Name Toaster Oven

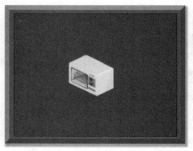

Cost: §100

Motive: Hunger (1)

Notes: This little roaster is better at starting fires than cooking food. Improve your Cooking Skills and buy a real oven. Until then, use a microwave.

Positive Potential Microwave

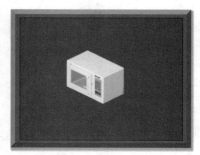

Cost: §250

Motive: Hunger (2)

Notes: You can warm up your food without burning the house down.

Dialectric Free Standing Range

Cost: §400

Motive: Hunger (5)

Notes: After raising your Cooking Skills to three or above, you can create nutritious (and satisfying) meals on this stove.

The "Pyrotorre" Gas Range

Cost: §1,000

Motive: Hunger (7)

Notes: A skilled chef can create works of art on this stove.

NOTE

Although an expensive stove enhances your Sim meals, it is only one of three steps in the cooking process. To maximize the potential of your stove, you need an excellent refrigerator for storage, and a food processor for efficient preparation.

Wild Bill THX-451 Barbecue

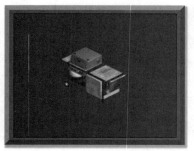

Cost: §350

Motive: Hunger (4)

Notes: Only experienced adult chefs should fire up the barbecue. Be careful not to position the grill near flammable items.

XLR8R Food Processor

Cost: §220

Motive: Hunger (2)

Notes: A food processor speeds up meal preparation and enhances food quality.

Junk Genie Trash Compactor

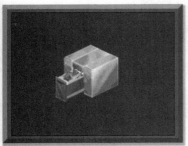

Cost: §375

Motive: None

Notes: A compactor holds more garbage than a trash can, and even when it is full, it will not degrade the Room rating because the trash is concealed.

Dish Duster Deluxe

Cost: §550

Motive: Dirty dishes lower your Room score.

Notes: Kids can't use the dishwasher, but it still cuts cleanup time considerably, and the countertop can be used for placing other items (sorry, no eating allowed).

Fuzzy Logic Dishwasher

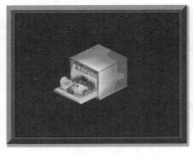

Cost: §950

Motive: Dirty dishes lower your Room score.

Notes: The Cadillac of dishwashers cleans up kitchen messes in a snap. This model has fewer breakdowns than the Dish Duster.

Llamark Refrigerator

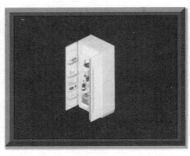

Cost: §600

Motive: Hunger (6)

Notes: This model is sufficient while your Sims are building up their Cooking Skills.

Porcina Refrigerator Model P1g-S

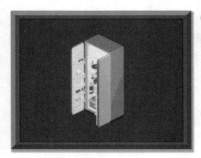

Cost: §1,200

Motive: Hunger (7)

Notes: This model produces more satisfying food for your Sims.

Freeze Secret Refrigerator

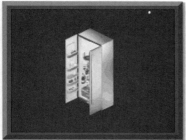

Cost: §2,500

Motive: Hunger (8)

Notes: The best place to store your food. When it's matched with a food processor, gas stove, and an experienced chef, your Sims will be licking their lips.

Plumbing

Sims can't carry buckets to the well for their weekly bath, and the outhouse hasn't worked in years, so install various plumbing objects to maintain a clean, healthy environment. Of course, not every plumbing object is essential, but you can't beat a relaxing hour in the hot tub with a few of your closest friends (or casual acquaintances).

Hydronomic Kitchen Sink

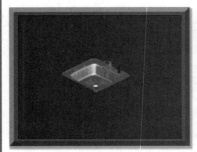

Cost: §250

Motive: Hygiene (2)

Notes: Without it the Sims would be washing dishes in the bathroom.

Epikouros Kitchen Sink

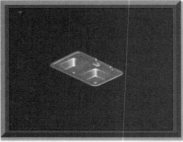

Cost: §500

Motive: Hygiene (3)

Notes: It's twice as big as the single, but a dishwasher is a better investment.

"Andersonville" Pedestal Sink

Cost: §400

Motive: Hygiene (2)

Notes: Neat Sims like to wash their hands after using the toilet.

Hygeia-O-Matic Toilet

Cost: §300

Motive: Bladder (8)

Notes: Hey, your only other option is the floor.

Flush Force 5 XLT

Cost: §1,200

Motives: Comfort (4), Bladder (8)

Notes: Your Sims can't go to the ballpark to get a good seat, but they can sit in a lap of luxury in the bathroom.

SpaceMiser Shower

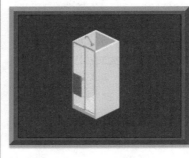

Cost: §650

Motive: Hygiene (6)

Notes: This is basic equipment in a Sims bathroom. One Sim can shower at a time, and the neat ones tend to linger longer than the sloppy ones. Sims are generally shy if they are not in love with a housemate, so you may need more than one shower (and bathroom) to prevent a traffic jam in the bathroom.

Justa Bathtub

Cost: §800

Motives: Comfort (3), Hygiene (6)

Notes: Your Sims get a double benefit from a relaxing bath when they have a little extra time.

Sani-Queen Bathtub

Cost: §1,500

Motives: Comfort (5), Hygiene (8)

Notes: Almost twice the price, but the added Comfort and Hygiene points are worth it.

Hydrothera Bathtub

Cost: §3,200

Motives: Comfort (8), Hygiene (10)

Notes: The most fun a Sim can have alone. Save your Simoleans, buy it, and listen to sounds of relaxation.

WhirlWizard Hot Tub

Cost: §6,500

Motives: Comfort (6), Hygiene (2), Fun (2)

Notes: Up to four adult Sims can relax, mingle, and begin lasting relationships in the hot tub.

Lighting

Sims love natural light, so make sure the sun shines through your windows from every direction. And, when the sun goes down, your Sims need plenty of lighting on the walls, floors, and tables to illuminate their world until bedtime. Although only three lamps listed below have direct impact on the Room score, all of the lamps have a collective effect when spread evenly throughout the home. Pay special attention to key activity areas in the kitchen, family room, bedrooms, and of course, the bathroom.

CAUTION

Lamp bulbs burn out with use, and they must be replaced. Sims can replace their own bulbs, but without Mechanical Skills, they run the risk of electrocution. Hiring a repairman is another option, but at §50 per hour, this can be very costly.

Table Lamps

Bottle Lamp

Cost: §25

Motive: None

Love n' Haight Lava Lamp

Cost: §80

Motive: Room (2)

Ceramiche Table Lamp

Cost: §85

Motive: None

Elite Reflections Chrome Lamp

Cost: §180

Motive: None

SC Electric Co. Antique Lamp

Cost: §300

Motive: Room (1)

Floor Lamps

Halogen Heaven Lamp by Contempto

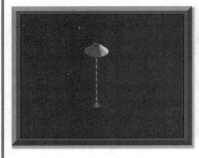

Cost: §50

Motive: None

Lumpen Lumeniat Floor Lamp

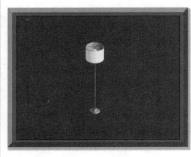

Cost: §100

Motive: None

Torchosteronne Floor Lamp

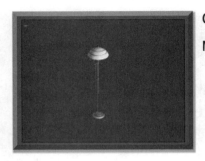

Cost: §350

Motive: Room (1)

Wall Lamps

White Globe Sconce

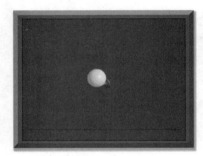

Cost: §35

Motive: None

Oval Glass Sconce

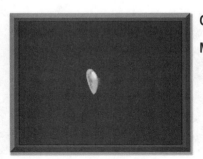

Cost: §85

Motive: None

Top Brass Sconce

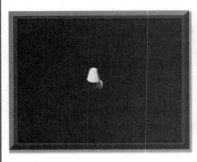

Cost: §110

Motive: None

Blue Plate Special Sconce

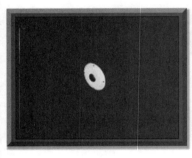

Cost: §135

Motive: None

Outside Lamp

Garden Lamp (Outdoor Use Only)

Cost: §50

Motive: None

Miscellaneous

We're down to the objects that are hard to fit into a category—everything from bookcases to beverage bars. Don't make the mistake of ignoring these items because you think they're luxuries; your Sim's life would be extremely difficult without a trash can, alarm clock, and bookcase. Plus, if you want to improve your Sim's Charisma and Body ratings, you'll need a mirror and exercise machine. So, once you install the basic objects in your house, look to the Miscellaneous category for objects that take your Sim's lifestyle to the next level.

SnoozMore Alarm Clock

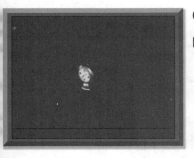

Cost: §30

Motive: None

Notes: After you set the clock, it will ring two hours before the carpool arrives for every working Sim in your house.

Trash Can

Cost: §30

Motive: None

Notes: Without a place to put trash, your Sim house will become a fly-infested hovel.

Magical Mystery Toy Box

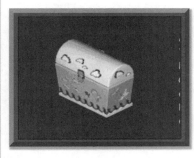

Cost: §50

Motive: Fun (2)

Notes: A good entertainment alternative if your kids are getting bleary-eyed in front of the computer.

Narcisco Wall Mirror

Cost: §100

Motive: Improves Charisma

Notes: Adults can Practice speech in front of the mirror to improve their Charisma.

Medicine Cabinet

Cost: §125

Motive: Hygiene (1), Improves Charisma

Notes: Your Sims can Practice speech in the bathroom and improve their Hygiene at the same time.

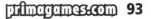

Narcisco Floor Mirror

Cost: §150

Motive: Improves Charisma

Notes: Place this mirror anywhere to practice Charisma without locking other Sims out of the bathroom.

Will Lloyd Wright Doll House

Cost: §180

Motive: Fun (2)

Notes: An engaging group activity for kids and adults.

Cheap Pine Bookcase

Cost: §250

Motive: Fun (1), Improve Cooking, Mechanical, and Study Skills

Notes: Reading books is the best way to prevent premature death from fires or electrocution.

"Dimanche" Folding Easel

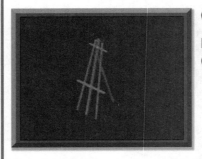

Cost: §250

Motive: Fun (2), Improves Creativity

Notes: With practice, a Sim can improve Creativity, and eventually sell a picture for up to §166.

Pinegulcher Dresser

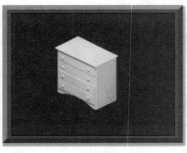

Cost: §250

Motive: None

Notes: A Sim can change into various formal, work, and leisure outfits, and even acquire a new body type.

Kinderstuff Dresser

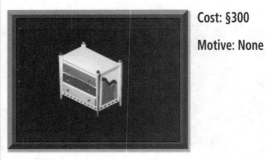

Cost: §300

Motive: None

Notes: Kids like to dress up too!

Amishim Bookcase

Cost: §500

Motive: Fun (2), Improves Cooking, Mechanical, and Study Skills

Notes: This expensive bookcase awards Skill points at the same rate as the cheaper one.

Chuck Matewell Chess Set

Cost: §500

Motive: Fun (2), Improves Logic

Notes: Serious Sims gain the most Fun points by playing, and any two Sims can improve Logic by playing each other.

Traditional Oak Armoire

Cost: §550

Motive: Room (1)

Notes: This dresser allows your Sim to change clothes (body skins). The choices vary, depending upon the Sim's current outfit.

SuperDoop Basketball Hoop

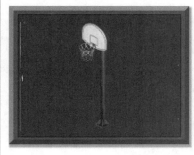

Cost: §650

Motive: Fun (4)

Notes: Active Sims love to play hoops, and any visitor is welcome to join the fun. A Sim with higher Body points performs better on the court.

"Exerto" Benchpress Exercise Machine

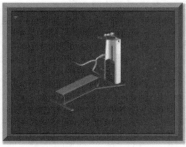

Cost: §700

Motive: Improves Body

Notes: Adult Sims can bulk up their Body points with exercise sessions.

Bachman Wood Beverage Bar

Cost: §800

Motive: Hunger (1), Fun (3), Room (2)

Notes: Every drink lowers the Bladder score, but adult Sims like to make drinks for themselves and friends. Kids can grab a soda from the fridge.

Libri di Regina Bookcase

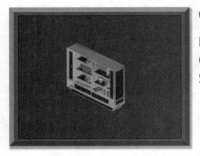

Cost: §900

Motive: Fun (3), Improves Cooking, Mechanical, and Study Skills

Notes: This stylish bookcase is perfect for a swanky Sim pad, but it still imparts Skill points at the same rate as the pine model.

Antique Armoire

Cost: §1,200

Motive: Room (2)

Notes: A more expensive version of the cheaper armoire, but it adds twice as many Room points.

The Funinator Deluxe

Cost: §1,200

Motive: Fun (5)

Notes: When the house is swarming with kids, send them outside to raise their Fun bar and burn some energy.

Chimeway & Daughters Piano

Cost: §3,500

Motive: Fun (4), Room (3), Improves Creativity

Notes: The most creative Sims will produce more beautiful music. The better the music, the greater the chance that listeners will like it. If a listener does not like the music, both Sims' Relationship scores will deteriorate.

Aristoscratch Pool Table

Cost: §4,200

Motive: Fun (6)

Notes: Up to two Sims use the table at the same time. Make sure that you allow enough room for Sims to get to the table and walk around it during play.

CHAPTER 7:
ALL IN THE FAMILY

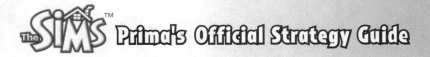

Introduction

Up to this point, we've covered the mechanics of *The Sims*. By now you should be familiar with creating families, building houses, buying objects, and getting jobs; and you should have considerable insight into how a Sim thinks and acts. Now, let's put it all together and join several Sim households in action. In this chapter we introduce you to working Sims families, ranging from one-Sim homes to larger households with kids and babies. Finally, we take an in-depth look at one of the toughest challenges in *The Sims*: building positive (and long-lasting) Relationships.

You Can Make It Alone

The biggest difficulty in being a bachelor is that you have to do everything yourself (sounds like real life, doesn't it?). You'll need to cook, clean, and improve your Skills, while at the same time keep up with a work schedule and satisfy your personal Motives. There's always time for Fun, and a good sofa or easy chair will provide a measure of Comfort. However, it's impossible to socialize while at work, and you will be frustrated watching neighbors drop by during the day and then leave when no one answers the door.

The Single Sim's Career

As a lone Sim you must choose a job that has decent hours and light friendship demands. This leaves a Military career as your only option. At most levels you work a six-hour day, and you won't need a single friend for the first five levels. A promotion to Level 6 requires one friend, but that can be established after you refine your schedule.

Designing a Bachelor Pad

There are several considerations when designing and furnishing a house for one Sim. Review the following checklist before you place your first wall stake.

Fig. 7-1. It's hardly the lap of luxury, but you have everything you need to get a job, keep your sanity, and learn how to cook.

- **Keep your house small, and place the front door close to the street. This allows you to milk a few extra minutes out of every morning before meeting the car pool.**

- **The interior should include a bedroom, bathroom, and living room. Rather than add a family room, use an outside patio area for Fun objects and an exercise machine. A Military career requires an ever-increasing number of Body Skill points.**

- **Install only enough counter space to place a food processor and prepare your meals. This leaves more space for a table and chairs. Buy at least two chairs so that you can socialize with a friend while sharing a meal.**

- **Without the space or the budget to buy expensive sofas or recliners, get a top-of-the-line bed, which enables your Sim to get by on fewer hours of sleep. Buy an inexpensive nightstand for an alarm clock, and add a few wall lights to boost your Room score.**

- **You'll need a computer for your job search, but keep in mind that you can return it within 24 Sim-hours for a full refund. Find your Military job and then pack up the PC.**

- **Buy an expensive refrigerator to maximize the quality of your food, but don't bother with a stove until your Sim learns how to cook.**

- **Because of your career, there's no need to socialize until you are up for promotion to Level 6, so don't waste money on living room chairs or an expensive sofa. A cheap TV will provide enough Fun for now.**

Leaving the Single Life

Eventually you will tire of the solitary lifestyle, which, thanks to the romantic tendencies of most Sims, is not a problem. The first step is friendship. After the Relationship bar tops 70, your Sim needs to lay on the romance, with plenty of kissing and hugging. Eventually, the Propose option will appear on the menu.

Fig. 7-2. The kissin' and huggin' pays off; now it's time to pop the question.

A marriage proposal can only take place in the home of the proposer, so set the mood (you know, empty your Bladder somewhere other than on the floor, clean up yesterday's dishes, and hide those overdue bills). After accepting the proposal, your new spouse moves into your place, along with a good job (a good thing) and plenty of money (a really good thing). But, proposing does not guarantee a positive response. For example, a Sim will never accept the proposal on an empty stomach, so you might want to eat dinner first.

Fig. 7-3. "We're alone, the time is perfect, and I've got grass stains on my knee."

Fig. 7-4. "Nope, sorry, I can't marry you on an empty stomach. Besides, your current lover is hiding in the bushes."

Keep in mind that you have to create potential mates, because the game won't provide them. You might as well choose compatible personalities, and it doesn't hurt to spend some time on career development. Remember that another Sim can also propose to you in his or her house; so unless you want to change residences, hold the romantic interludes at your place.

NOTE

After marriage, your Sim will still share a bed with any other Sim with a high enough Friendship score (over 70), so don't be surprised if your Sim ends up on the couch when his buddy beats him to the sack.

Fig. 7-5. When two Sims decide to get married, they change clothes and complete the ceremony within seconds.

A three-way relationship makes it easier to have babies. Not only are there additional combinations for procreation, but you can also have one of the working adults take a night job, so there is a caregiver for the baby during the day. Even with staggered schedules, there will be at least one sleepless Sim until the baby matures, so don't get too complacent with this arrangement.

Interestingly, if your future spouse already has children, and at least one adult still resides in his or her original house, the kids stay. So, your new spouse arrives with job and bank account intact, sans kids. What a deal!

That isn't the only unusual aspect of married life in Sims-ville. Marriage is not sacred here, at least not in the legal sense. A Sim can have multiple mates all living under the same roof, as pictured in figure 7-6. The interpersonal dynamics can sometimes get a little dicey, but it's workable, and the extra income is great!

Married, with Children

After your Sims promise undying love and devotion to each other (or, at least until the next promotion), it's time to have a baby. Actually, your Sims can live together for years without having children, but if they do, you'll be missing one of the *The Sims'* most vexing experiences.

Conception

The exercise of making a baby is similar to the steps taken to activate the marriage Proposal option. First, get a male and female Sim together, and then concentrate on strengthening their relationship. When both Sims are obviously enjoying each other's company, lay on the hugs and kisses. Keep smooching until you receive the option to have a baby, as pictured in figure 7-7.

Fig. 7-6. After the wedding, our Sim bride goes to bed with her former boyfriend.

Fig. 7-7. A little bundle of joy is just a click away.

If you answer yes, a bassinet appears almost instantly, amid an explosion of dandelions. The happy couple celebrates the new arrival, then they quickly go back to their daily routine. This baby thing is a snap. Well, not exactly.

Fig. 7-8. Yippee! It's a boy!

In short order, the little bundle of joy starts screaming. A Sim will eventually respond to the cries, but rather than wait, get someone to the baby immediately. Clicking on the bassinet reveals three options: Feed, Play, or Sing. When in doubt, feed the baby, but be prepared to come right back with Play or Sing when the baby starts wailing again.

Fig. 7-9. Kids do a great job entertaining the baby during one of its frequent crying sessions.

This mayhem continues for three Sim days, during which time the household will be in an uproar. Forget about getting eight hours of beauty sleep. Designate one Sim as primary caregiver, preferably one who does not work, because the baby's cries wake any Sim in the room. The first day is nonstop crying. By the second day, the baby sleeps for a few hours at a time; take advantage of the break and send the caregiver to bed. As long as you stay responsive, the baby evolves into a runny-nosed kid, and the family can get back to normal. However, if you spend too much time in the hot tub and not enough time with the baby, a social service worker will march into your house and take the baby, as pictured in figure 7-10. You'll only receive one warning, so don't take this responsibility lightly.

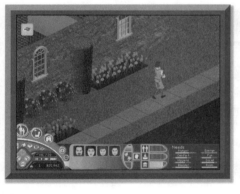

Fig. 7-10. We hardly knew the little tyke!

NOTE

The bassinet appears near the spot where your Sims made the decision to have a baby. Although the Sims cannot move the bassinet, you can use the Hand Tool to move it. Pick a location that is isolated from other sleeping areas, so the disturbance is kept to a minimum.

Building and Maintaining Healthy Relationships

Gathering an ever-increasing number of friends is critical for career advancement, especially at the higher levels. It is also your Sims' only way to build up their Social scores and fend off frequent bouts of depression. In this section we outline the steps required for finding potential friends, building up positive feelings, and then maintaining healthy relationships.

Talk Is Cheap

The easiest way to make friends is often overlooked, because it is uneventful compared to other social events. However, you can almost always initiate a conversation between Sims (regardless of their Friendship scores), and keep it going for a very long time. During this benign exchange of thought balloons, you can usually nudge the Friendship score in a positive direction. When starting from 0 it takes a few encounters to get over 50 (true friendship), but once you reach this threshold, the action picks up considerably. Our newly married Sims went from a score of 64 to a marriage proposal in one evening. Although the woman eventually declined because her stomach was growling, she proposed the next day and the marriage was consummated.

Fig. 7-11. Keep talking and your Friendship score will grow.

Finding Time to Socialize

After your Sim starts working, it's difficult to find time to call other Sims and arrange meetings. Mornings are worst, although you have more options if your neighborhood has several non-working Sims. Your best bet is to start socializing right after coming home from work. Take care of personal needs first—Hygiene and Bladder—and then "Serve Dinner." Don't let a bad chef get near the stove; you can't afford to waste time putting out a fire or your guests will leave. With a counter full of food, your friends head straight for the kitchen, where you can chat over a plate of Sim-grub and then plan the rest of your evening.

Positive Social Events

After everyone is finished eating, take a little time for pleasant conversation. In the case of the female Sims pictured in figure 7-11, there is a lot of fence mending to accomplish, because one just stole the other's love interest. But, Sims are generally forgiving, and a quarrel can be mended with a few drinks, a game of pool, or a long soak in the hot tub.

Ideally, your house has an entertainment room with group activity items such as a pool table, stereo, or beverage bar. After you get everyone into the room, keep them busy with a string of activities. Even our former lovers can't resist a dance when the music starts playing, as pictured in figure 7-12.

Fig. 7-12. Our Sim guy is enjoying this dance with his former girlfriend, although his current wife will probably slap him when the music stops playing (if she can stay awake long enough).

CAUTION

Avoid close activities such as dancing, hugging, etc. when the current spouse or love interest is in the room. When the dance was over (figure 7-12), our Sim wife did indeed slap her new husband, causing her recently mended Relationship score with the other woman to drop from +14 to –7.

One of the most difficult aspects of entertaining in the evening is keeping the host from falling asleep on the floor. After a hard day's work, most Sims begin nodding out around 10:00 p.m. You can squeeze a little extra time out of the evening if they take a short nap after coming home from work. Be prepared for a grouchy Sim in the morning (figure 7-13) if the evening's festivities stretch too far into the night.

Fig. 7-13. Our tired party girl hurries off to the car pool without a shower— not a good way to impress her superiors.

TIP

After your guests arrive, you need to micromanage your Sims so they don't go off and take care of their own needs. Obviously, you must pay attention to a full Bladder, but you can delay other actions by redirecting your Sims to group activities. Break up the party when your Sims are teetering on the edge of exhaustion or they'll fall asleep on the floor.

CAUTION

Visiting Sims generally hang around until 1:00 a.m. or later, which is undoubtedly past your bedtime. Direct your Sims to bed at the appropriate time, or they may feel compelled to hang out with their guests until well past midnight, as pictured in figure 7-14.

Fig. 7-14. Our host Sim is still cleaning up dishes when he should be asleep.

Stockpiling Potential Friends

When your career advances to the top promotion level, you need more than 10 friends in every career except the Military. Hence, it's a good idea to create a few additional families early in the game, and you might want to fill one house with the maximum of eight Sims to dramatically increase your pool.

Visitors Coming and Going

The following tables include important information on how and why visitors do the things they do. You may not be able to directly control your guests' actions, but at least you won't take it personally when they decide to split.

Visitors' Starting Motives

MOTIVE	STARTING VALUE
Bladder	0 to 30
Comfort	30 to 70
Energy	35
Fun	-20 to 20
Hunger	-30 to -20
Hygiene	90
Social	-50 to -40

In a perfect Sim-world, visitors leave your house just past 1:00 a.m. However if one of their Motives falls into the danger zone, they will depart earlier. When this happens, the Sim's thought balloon reveals a reason for the early exit.

Visitors' Leaving Motives

MOTIVE	DROPS BELOW THIS VALUE
Bladder	-90
Comfort	-70
Energy	-80
Fun	-55
Hunger	-50
Hygiene	-70
Mood	-75
Room	-100
Social	-85

Guest Activities

There are three types of visitor activities: those initiated by a family member, shared activities, and autonomous activities where guests are on their own. The following sections and tables describe each type.

Activities Initiated by Family Member

One of the Sims under your control must prepare food or turn on the TV before visitors can join in. Turning on the TV takes a second, but you need a little prep time for a meal. It's a good idea to begin meal preparation immediately after inviting friends over.

Shared Activities

A Sim can start any of the following activities and then invite the participation of a guest.

OBJECT	VISITORS' INVOLVEMENT
Basketball Hoop	Join
Chess	Join
Dollhouse	Watch
Hot Tub	Join
Pinball Machine	Join
Play Structure	Join
Piano	Watch
Pool Table	Join
Stereo	Join, Dance
Train Set	Watch

Autonomous Activities

Visiting Sims can begin any of the following activities on their own.

Visitors' Autonomous Activities

OBJECT	AUTONOMOUS ACTION
Aquarium	Watch Fish
Baby	Play
Bar	Have a Drink
Chair	Sit
Chair (Recliner)	Sit
Coffee (Espresso Machine)	Drink Espresso
Coffeemaker	Drink Coffee
Fire	Panic
Flamingo	View
Fountain	Play
Lava Lamp	View
Painting	View
Pool	Swim
Pool Diving Board	Dive In
Pool Ladder	Get In/Out
Sculpture	View
Sink	Wash Hands
Sofa	Sit
Toilet	Use, Flush
Tombstone/Urn	Mourn
Toy Box	Play
Trash Can (Inside)	Dispose

Social Interactions

The results of various interactions are best learned by experience because of the individual personality traits that come into play. However, it helps to have an idea what each action may produce. The following table offers notes on each interaction.

INTERACTION	DESCRIPTION
Back Rub	When well-received, it is a good transition into kissing and hugging, but the Relationship score should already be over 50.
Brag	This is what mean Sims do to your Sim. Don't use it, unless you want to ruin a good friendship.
Compliment	Generally positive, but you should withhold compliments until your Relationship score is above 15.
Dance	Great activity between friends (40+), but it almost always causes a jealous reaction from a jilted lover.
Entertain	A somewhat goofy activity, but it usually works well with other Playful Sims.
Fight	Don't do it (unless you know you can take the other Sim!).
Flirt	A great way to boost a strong Relationship (70+) into the serious zone, but watch your back. Flirting usually triggers a jealous reaction from significant others.
Give Gift	A benign way to say you like the other Sim, or that you're sorry for acting like an idiot at the last party; best used with 40+ Relationship scores.
Hug	This one's always fun if the hug-ee's Relationship score is +60; a good transition to kisses, and then a marriage proposal.
Joke	Good between casual friends (+15) who are both Playful.
Kiss	The relationship is heating up, but if a jealous ex or current lover is in the vicinity, someone could get slapped.
Talk	The starting point of every friendship.
Tease	Why bother, unless you don't like the other Sim.
Tickle	Not as positive as it might seem, but Playful Sims are definitely more receptive.

CHAPTER 8:
A DAY IN THE LIFE

Introduction

Now, it's time to turn on our Sim-Cam and follow a few of our families as they handle the ups and downs of Sim life. In this chapter we switch to a scrapbook format, with screenshots of our Sims in interesting—and sometimes compromising—situations. Admittedly, we coaxed our Sims into some of these dilemmas. But it's all in fun, and we think it's the best way for you to get a feel for this amazing game.

As the Sim Turns

Five o'clock wakeup call is not pretty. Even with full Energy bars, your Sims can be a little cranky, but don't give them any slack. Get the best chef into the kitchen pronto, to serve Breakfast for everyone in the house.

Switching to Zoomed Out view is a good way to manage the household early in the morning. This way you can quickly target important tasks for completion before the car pool arrives.

Our third adult roommate, Mortimer, just returned home from his night shift, so for now, his needs are secondary. We put him to work mopping the kitchen floor (the dishwasher broke last night, but everyone was falling asleep, so we figured it would keep until morning).

Before we are accused of being sexist, we should explain that the only reason Bella is cooking for everyone is that she is the most experienced chef. If Mark turns on the stove, chances are the kitchen will burn down. We promise to boost his Cooking Skills at the first opportunity.

Mark is, well, busy at the moment. It's too bad he doesn't gain Energy points for sitting on the toilet, because he stayed up much too late last night. A good breakfast helps, but getting through the day won't be easy, and he can forget about any promotions thanks to his sub-par mood.

It's a nice family breakfast with husband Mortimer on the left, wife Bella on the right, and Bella's ex-boyfriend Mark in the middle. However, there isn't much time for chitchat, because the car pool has arrived, and it will leave at a few minutes past nine.

After canceling his thoughts about sleeping, we click on Mark's car pool. He changes clothes faster than Superman and sprints to his ride in the nick of time. Have a nice day, Mark!

Bella is on her way to the car pool and we have about a half hour to get Mark in gear, which may be a problem due to his low Energy rating. Unfortunately, Bella's Hygiene leaves much to be desired. We make a mental note to get her into the shower before bedtime tonight so she'll be fresh as a daisy in the mornin).

Poor Mortimer! We've been so focused on getting Bella and Mark to work, we didn't notice that the poor slob is asleep on his feet! We need to wake him up (he'll be so happy), and send him to bed.

Uh-oh, big time problem with Mark. He's standing in the kitchen in his pajamas, in a catatonic state. With only a half hour to get to the car pool, we need to shake him up a little and point him to the door.

We receive a reminder that Mortimer's car pool arrives at 4:00 p.m. Unfortunately we forgot to set his alarm, and his Hygiene and Bladder bars have gone south, so we need to wake him up soon. Fortunately, he ate before bedtime, so he can probably get by without a big meal.

Mortimer is up and he's not happy. With the amount of time remaining before his car pool shows up, he can empty his bladder and get in half a shower before racing out the door.

Mark is well rested, so he can fend for himself this morning. He steps into the shower as the car pool arrives, so he has almost one hour to get ready. But, while in the shower, he decides to take the day off and join Bella.

With Mortimer out of the house, we can concentrate on Bella and Mark, who have both arrived home from work. Mark socialized a little too much the night before, so he went straight to bed without any prompting.

The three housemates share a pleasant breakfast together. Perhaps they have finally buried the hatchet after the Mortimer-Bella-Mark thing. We can only hope.

Mortimer arrives home at 1:00 a.m.. After a bathroom break and quick shower, we send him straight to bed so he can party with Bella tomorrow, who has decided to take the day off.

Mark grabs the phone to invite a friend over, but before he can dial, a local radio station calls with great news. He just won §550 in a promotion!

Mark calls a friend, who says he'll be right over. While Mark changes into his Speedo, Mortimer, Jeff, and Bella enjoy a dip in the pool. That's right, Mortimer missed his car pool, too. It's a day off (without pay) for the entire house!

After dinner, Jeff heads for home. Bella and Mark retreat to the den, where Bella rubs Mark's back.

It's on to the hot tub for a long, relaxing soak. Comfort, Hygiene, Social, and Fun scores are soaring. It's too bad we have to eat and empty our Bladders or we'd never leave!

One good rub deserves a hug, as things suddenly heat up between the former lovers.

Everyone will be hungry after the swim and soak, so Bella hops out to make dinner. Soon, everyone grabs a plate and starts discussing what life will be like when they are all unemployed. Everyone, that is, except Mortimer, who prefers standing.

Mortimer takes one look at the lip-locked Sims and heads straight for the bar.

After a couple of adult beverages, Mortimer follows the lovers into the hallway where they are still groping each other like teenagers on prom night.

Bella drives off to work while our two Sim-Neanderthals take their fight to the bathroom.

What will become of our star-crossed lovers?

Will Bella leave Mortimer and go back to Mark?

Will Mark feel guilty about wrecking Mortimer's marriage, and move in with the Newbies?

Will Bella reveal what she and Jeff were really doing in the hot tub?

Who will clean up the bathroom?

For the answers to these burning questions, stay tuned for the next episode of...*As the Sim Turns.*

Mortimer shows his frustration by slapping Mark across the cheek (he's such an animal). Bella is disgusted and goes upstairs to bed.

Life with the Pleasants

One slap turns to another and seven hours later, Mortimer and Mark are still duking it out.

Jeff experiences the joys of working a night shift— cleaning up his family's dinner dishes...

...and taking out the trash at four in the morning.

Skeeter misses one too many days of school and gets the bad news—he's on his way to military school, never to be seen again.

Everyone is asleep, so Jeff takes an opportunity to practice his Charisma in front of the bathroom mirror. Unfortunately for Jeff, the walking dead also take this opportunity to float through the mirror and scare the •&$%$# out of him.

Although his icon has already disappeared from the control panel, Skeeter enjoys one last breakfast before he is exiled from the game.

Like all kids, Daniel and Skeeter can only make snacks on their own, so someone must serve their breakfast before school.

Not wanting to follow in his brother's footsteps, Daniel hits the books and improves his grades.

Hmmm. Which pile should I pay first, the red one or the yellow one? Get a clue, Jeff—if you don't pay the red ones, they'll repossess your furniture!

The Maid should get riot pay for all the garbage this family leaves on the floor!

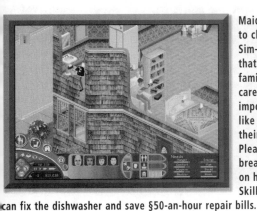

Maids are limited to cleaning up Sim-messes, but that frees up the family to take care of other important needs, like advancing their skills. Diane Pleasant takes a break to bone up on her Mechanical Skills. Perhaps she can fix the dishwasher and save §50-an-hour repair bills.

Pity the Poor Bachelor

With garbage a foot thick on the floor of his house, our bachelor decides to stay outside and entertain a new lady friend with his juggling act.

"Wow, she really likes me! Maybe she won't notice the garbage if I invite her inside."

"I really like you Bella, so I got you a pair of basketball shoes!"

Bachelors on a fixed budget can have a difficult time having fun. A basketball hoop in the back yard is a good investment, and if you can find a Playful friend, it's a cheap date, too.

"Excuse me, son, could you please move out of the fire so I can extinguish it?"

Kids Are People, Too

Armed with a new gas stove and absolutely no cooking ability, this bachelor decides to flame-broil the kitchen.

Toy boxes are small and relatively inexpensive. If they are placed in the bedroom, your kids can sneak in a little Fun time before school.

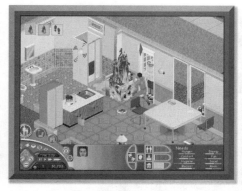

Whew, the fireman is here to put out the fire. There's only one problem: he can't get into the house because our hero is standing in front of the stove, which happens to be next to the door. We understand that the bachelor's quarters are tight, but it's probably not a good idea to put the stove next to the front door. By the time the fireman makes his way to the back door, your bachelor could be toast.

Children have fewer inhibitions, but they still don't like to use the bathroom in front of the Maid or their siblings.

Skeeter and Matthew enjoy a little Social and Fun time playing with their railroad town.

Left to their own devices, kids often stay up long past the time their parents hit the sack. In fact, even with Free Will activated, parents feel no responsibility for getting their children to bed early. So, if you forget to send the kids to bed, get ready for some serious tantrums in the morning.

Unlike the railroad, the pinball machine is a solo activity.

Skillful Sims

An exercise machine is the obvious choice for improving a Sim's Body Skill, but if you can keep your Sims in the pool, they'll increase Body scores even faster, and boost Fun at the same time.

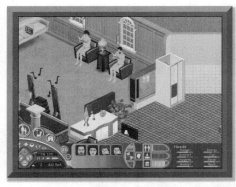

Unlike adults, who need toys for their playtime, kids can play with each other.

Sometimes it can be hard to get your Sims to slow down long enough for serious Skill enhancement, especially if it means sitting down to read. The solution is simple: Place two comfortable chairs close to the bookcase, and give each Sim different Skill assignments. Remember that you only need one Cooking expert and one Mechanical expert in the same house. Divide reading assignments appropriately to bring their Skills quickly up to speed.

You might be concerned about an adult male who stands for hours in front of a full-length mirror in his Speedo. However, it makes sense to place a mirror in the family room for easier access. This way, your Sims won't tie up the bathroom practicing Charisma in the mirror over the sink.

Increasing the Creativity Skill through painting has an added bonus—the ability to sell your painting. But, don't get too excited; a bad painting fetches only §1 on the open market.

With minimal Mechanical Skill, repairing this shower seems to take forever, and all the while, Mark's Comfort and Energy scores are dropping. Maybe a Repairman is worth the price until Mark earns a few more Mechanical points.

As the Sim Turns: Part Two

As we return to our Sim soap, Mortimer has just returned from another night shift, and after a light snack, he decides to take an early morning swim, thinking that Mark and Bella are busy getting ready for work. After swimming a few laps, he is ready to go to bed, but wait...where is the ladder?

"I can't get out of the pool!" says Mortimer, frantically. "I'll just tread water for a while until Mark or Bella come out. If I can just...keep... going...getting tired...so tired...."

Mark and Bella finally come outside, but it's too late. Poor Mortimer, exhausted and confused, has already dropped like a stone to the bottom of the pool.

After Mortimer's body is removed from the pool, a tombstone is erected on the spot where the ladder used to be. If Mortimer were still here, he would have appreciated the humor...maybe not.

After getting over the initial shock, Mark and Bella grieve at the site where their "friend" died.

"O.K., enough grieving," says Bella, as she tells Mark a real knee-slapper.

After some welcome comic relief, the two mourners console each other with a supportive hug. Right.

Then, they console each other further...with a dance?

Thinking the time is right (and that they have carried on the charade long enough), Mark pulls Bella close for a kiss. But, much to Mark's surprise, Bella suddenly cools and pushes him away.

What is this strange turn of events?

Did Bella entice Mark into helping her solve the "Mortimer" problem, only to leave him in the lurch?

Find the answers on the next episode of *As the Sim Turns*, on a computer near you!

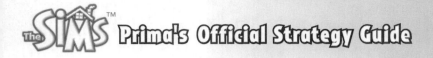

Sims in the Kitchen

In the Motives chapter, we provided a basic explanation of how Sims satisfy their Hunger score. As you know by now, food is readily available in the refrigerator, 24 hours a Sim-day. The supply is endless, and you never have to go to the market. However, the difference between what is in the refrigerator and what a Sim actually eats lies in the preparation. The following screens take you through the various options available to a Sim chef, and the table at the end of this chapter explains how the different appliances and countertops modify the quality of each meal.

After processing the food, Bella throws it in a pot and works her magic. Two more modifiers are at work here: Bella's Cooking Skill and the special features of the Pyrotorre Gas Range.

The snack, a §5 bag of chips, is the lowest item on the Sim food chain. It's better than nothing when your Sim is racing around getting ready for the car pool, but it barely nudges the Hunger bar.

When the meal is finished, Bella places a stack of plates on the counter.

For a much more satisfying meal, direct the best chef in the house to Prepare a Meal. In this screen, Bella is getting ready to throw the raw ingredients into the food processor (a positive modifier, as noted in the table below). While one Sim prepares breakfast, you can assign the other Sims to menial labor, such as mopping or picking up garbage.

Thrilled that he doesn't have to eat his own tasteless slop, Mark grabs a plate from the counter.

Another option for preparing multiple portions is to call out for a pizza. This is a good choice for a Sim who has a low Cooking Skill. Rather than using the stove and setting the kitchen on fire, a telephone call and §40 will buy a hot pie, delivered to the door in an hour.

The Sims love their pizza, and they can't wait to set it down and grab a slice. So, don't be surprised if your Sim plops the carton down on the first available counter—even in the bathroom—and starts grazing.

How Appliances and Surfaces Affect Hunger Score

APPLIANCE/SURFACE	HUNGER POINTS ADDED TO MEAL
Dishwasher	5
Trash Compactor	5
Fridge (Llamark)	9
Toaster Oven	9 (plus Cooking Skill)
Fridge (Porcina)	12
Counter (Barcelona)	16
Counter (NuMica)	16
Counter (Tiled)	16
Fridge (Freeze Secret)	16
Microwave	16 (plus Cooking Skill)
Food Processor	32
Stove (Dialectric)	32 (plus 1.5 x Cooking Skill)
Stove (Pyrotorre)	48 (plus 1.5 x Cooking Skill)

CHAPTER 9:
SURVIVAL TIPS

Introduction

The beauty of playing *The Sims* is that everyone's experience is different. When you take a serious approach to shaping your family, the game can mirror your own life. However, if you mismanage your Sims, they can sink into despair, waving their little arms in the air over failed relationships, poor career decisions, or even a bad mattress. You can always delete your family and start over. But then you would never get that warm, fuzzy feeling that comes from turning your pitiful Sims' world into Shangri La.

This chapter is devoted to the *Sims* player who wants to go the distance and fight the good fight. Because most Sim problems can be traced back to one or more deficient Motive scores, we have arranged the following tips into separate Motive sections. Although some of the information is covered in other chapters, this is meant to be a quick-reference guide for times of crisis. Simply turn to the appropriate Motive and save your Sim's life with one of our game-tested tips.

Of course, you can also take a more devious approach to satisfying or altering your Sim's needs. Our Cheats section gives you a bundle of unofficial commands to rock your Sim's world. We take no responsibility for the results. (In other words, don't come crying to us if you stick your Sim in a room with no doors and he or she drops dead!).

Hunger

Maximize Food Quality and Preparation Time

For the best food quality, upgrade *all* appliances and countertops. Anything short of the most expensive refrigerator, countertop, stove, etc., reduces the potential Hunger value of your meals. Preparing a meal quickly is all about kitchen design. Align your objects in the order of preparation, beginning with the refrigerator, followed by the food processor (figure 9-1), and then ending with the stove (figure 9-2).

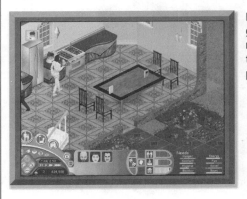

Fig. 9-1. The food goes from the refrigerator directly to the food processor.

Fig. 9-2. Next stop is the stove, right next door.

Have an open countertop next to the stove on the other side so the food preparer can set the plates down (figure 9-3). Although it has nothing to do with preparation, position the kitchen table and chairs close to the stove so that your Sims can grab their food, sit down together, and boost their Social scores (figure 9-4).

Fig. 9-5. After making dinner, our hard-working Sim can go to bed and sleep late in the morning.

Fig. 9-3. From the stove, the chef moves just a couple steps to the counter and sets down the plates.

After the food is on the counter, immediately send the Sim to bed. Most Sims should get up by 5, or the very latest, 6 a.m. to be on time for their morning jobs (the chef can sleep in). When everyone comes downstairs, breakfast (it's really dinner, but Sims don't care what you call it, as long as it doesn't have flies) will be on the counter (figure 9-6), fresh and ready to go. You'll save at least 20 Sim-minutes of morning prep time.

Fig. 9-4. If your Sims are prompted to eat, they'll be ready to grab a plate as soon as it hits the counter, and with the table nearby, they can eat, chat, and make it to work on time.

Designate one Sim as your chef. Make sure that Sim has easy access to a chair and bookcase, and then set aside time each day to Study Cooking. When the resident chef's Cooking Skill reaches 10, you have achieved the pinnacle of food preparation.

Make Breakfast the Night Before

Sim food lasts for at least seven hours before the flies arrive and the food is officially inedible. If you have one Sim in the house who doesn't work, have him or her prepare breakfast for everyone at around midnight, as pictured in figure 9-5.

Fig. 9-6. It's only 5:30 a.m., but our Sim kid is already eating breakfast. After taking care of his Hygiene, he'll still have time for studying or boosting his Fun score before the school bus arrives.

Comfort

When You Gotta Go, Go in Style

A toilet is often overlooked as a source of Comfort. The basic Hygeia-O-Matic Toilet costs only §300, but it provides zero Comfort. Spend the extra §900 and buy the Flush Force 5 XLT (figure 9-7). Your Sims have to use the bathroom anyway, so they might as well enjoy the +4 Comfort rating every time they take a seat.

Fig. 9-8. Our Sim is hungry, but he always has time to receive a nice Back Rub.

Fig. 9-7. You can live with a black-and-white TV for a while, but it doesn't make sense to do without the added comfort of the Flush Force.

Rub Your Sim the Right Way

Giving another Sim a Back Rub is a great way to increase your chances of seeing Hug, and eventually Kiss on the social interaction menu. However, don't forget that it also raises the recipient's Comfort level. If your Sim's Comfort level is down, even after a long night's sleep, try a few Back Rubs. It will send your Sim to work in a better mood, which might be just enough to earn the next promotion.

Hygiene

Your Mother Was Right

One of the biggest contributors to declining Hygiene is the lack of hand washing after using the bathroom (in the Sims and in real life). If your Sim does not have a Neat personality, you may need to initiate this action. If you keep it up throughout the day, your Sim will be in better shape in the morning, when a shorter shower can be the difference between making the car pool or missing a day of work.

Fig. 9-9. This Sim has an average Neat rating, which means she won't always wash her hands after using the bathroom. A few gentle reminders are in order.

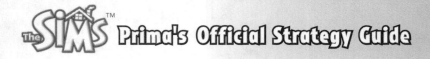
Flush Your Troubles Away

Sad but true, sloppy Sims don't flush (figure 9-10). It's easy to overlook this nasty habit during a busy day, but it could lead to trouble. A clogged toilet may not affect Hygiene directly, but if your Sim is forced to pee on the floor because the toilet is not working, the Hygiene score drops dramatically.

Fig. 9-10. Second time tonight for this soldier, and we're still waiting for the first flush.

Bladder

Sorry, there's no magic formula for relieving a full Bladder. However, to guard against emergencies and the resulting puddles on the floor, try building two semi-private stalls in your bathroom. This allows two Sims to use the facilities without infringing on each other's privacy, as pictured in figure 9-11.

Fig. 9-11. Dual stalls improve the traffic flow (and other flows) in the bathroom.

Energy
Getting Enough Sleep with Baby

Nothing drains a Sim's Energy bar faster than having a baby in the house (figure 9-12). If you want to survive the three-day baby period without everyone losing their jobs, you must sleep when the baby sleeps. Most likely, this will be in the middle of the day, because Sim babies, like their real counterparts, couldn't care less about their parents' sleep schedules. The baby will not sleep for a full eight hours; however, if you get five or six hours of sleep with the baby, you'll have enough Energy to carry out other important household tasks.

Fig. 9-12. This Sim mom is at the end of her rope, and the baby is just getting warmed up.

Kids Make Great Babysitters

It does nothing for their Fun or Social levels, but Sim kids will dutifully care for their baby siblings. When they come home from school, feed them, allow a short play period, and then lock them in the room with the baby (if you're feeling particularly sadistic, you can go into Build mode and wall them in). They usually respond on their own, but you can always direct them to the crib, as pictured in figure 9-13, (unless they are too exhausted and need sleep). Take advantage of this time by sending the regular caregiver to bed for some much-needed sleep.

Fig. 9-13. Big brother makes a great nanny.

Favorite Fun Activities

TRAIT	BEST ACTIVITIES
Neat	N/A
Outgoing	TV (Romance), Hot Tub, Pool (if Playful is also high)
Active	Basketball, Stereo (dance), Pool, TV (Action)
Lazy	TV (as long as it's on, they're happy!), Computer, Book
Playful	Any fun object, including Computer, Dollhouse, Train Set, VR Glasses, Pinball, etc. If also Active, shift to Basketball, Dance, and Pool.
Serious	Chess, Newspaper, Book, Paintings (just let them stare)
Nice	Usually up for anything
Mean	TV (Horror)

Fun

Finding the Right Activity for Your Sim

Unless your Sims live in a monastery, you should have plenty of Fun objects in your house. The trick is matching the right kind of activity with a Sim's personality. In the frenzy of daily schedules and maintaining Relationships, it's easy to lose touch with your Sim's personality traits. Visit the Personality menu often (click on the "head" icon) to review the five traits. Make sure you have at least one of the following objects readily available to your Sim (the bedroom is a good spot).

When in Doubt, Entertain Someone

If your Sim does not have access to a Fun activity, simply Entertain someone for an instant Fun (and Social) boost, as pictured in figure 9-14. You can usually repeat this activity several times, and it doesn't take much time (great for kids on busy school mornings).

A Sim should have at least six points (bars) in one of the following traits to maximize the recommended activity. Of course, an even higher number produces faster Fun rewards. To qualify for the opposite trait (e.g., Active/Lazy, Playful/Serious) a Sim should have no more than three points in the trait).

Fig. 9-14. When a good toy is not around, Sim kids love to Entertain each other.

Social

Satisfying Social requirements can be very frustrating, especially when Sims are on different work or sleep schedules. Socializing is a group effort, so plan small parties on a regular basis. Keep a notepad with all of your Sims' work schedules, so you know whom to invite at any time of the day.

- **It's O.K. to ask your guests to leave. After you shmooze a little and boost your Relationship score, send the Sim packing, and call up a different one. Use this round-robin approach to maintain all of your friendships.**

- **Don't let Mean Sims abuse you. This can be tough to control if you're not paying attention. When you're socializing with a Mean Sim, keep an eye on the activity queue in the screen's upper-left corner. If that Sim's head pops up (without you initiating it), it probably says "Be Teased by...," or "Be Insulted by...." Simply click on the icon to cancel the negative event and maintain your Relationship score. Once you diffuse the threat, engage the Sim in simple talking, or move your Sim into a group activity (pool table, hot tub, pool, etc.)**

- **Unless you like being the bad guy, don't advertise your advances toward one Sim if you already have a Relationship with another. Sims are extremely jealous, but you can still maintain multiple love relationships as long as you don't flaunt them in public.**

Room

A Room score crisis is easy to remedy. If you have the money, simply add more lights and paintings. Also check the quality of objects in the room, and upgrade whenever possible. If your room is jammed with expensive objects, lights, and paintings and your Room score is still low, there must be a mess somewhere. A normally maxed out Room score can slip with so much as a puddle on the floor (as pictured in figure 9-15). Clean up the mess to restore the Room score to its normal level.

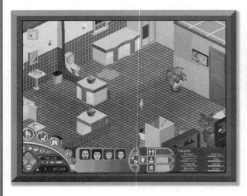

Fig. 9-15. It looks like someone fell short of the toilet. A mop will take care of the mess and raise the Room score.

Scan your house on a regular basis for the following negative Room factors:

- **Dead plants**
- **Cheap objects (especially furniture)**
- **Puddles (they can also indicate a bad appliance; when in doubt, click on the item to see if Repair comes up as an option)**
- **Dark areas**
- **If you have the money, replace items taken by the Repo guy.**

Cheats

Activate the cheat command line at any time during a game by pressing [Ctrl] + [Shift] + [C]. An input box appears in the screen's upper left corner. Type in one of the codes listed below. You must re-activate the command line after each cheat is entered. The following cheats work only with Version 1.1 or later of *The Sims*.

Cheats

DESCRIPTION	CODE INPUT
1,000 Simoleans	rosebud
Import and load specific FAM file	import <FAM file>
Create moat or streams	water_tool
Create-a-character mode	edit_char
Display personality and interests	interests
Draw all animation disabled	draw_all_frames off
Draw all animation enabled	draw_all_frames on
Execute "file.cht" file as a list of cheats	cht <filename>
Floorable grid disabled	draw_floorable off
Floorable grid enabled	draw_floorable on
Map editor disabled	map_edit off
Map editor enabled	map_edit on
Move any object (on)	move_objects on
Move any object (off)	move_objects off
Preview animations disabled	preview_anims off
Preview animations enabled	preview_anims on
Quit game	quit
Rotate camera	rotation <0-3>
Save currently loaded house	save
Save family history file	history
Selected person's path displayed	draw_routes on

DESCRIPTION	CODE INPUT
Selected person's path hidden	draw_routes off
Set event logging mask	log_mask
Set free thinking level	autonomy <1-100>
Set game speed	sim_speed <-1000-1000>
Set grass change value	edit_grass <number>:
Set grass growth	grow_grass <0-150>
Set maximum milliseconds to allow simulator	sim_limit <milliseconds>
Set sim speed	sim_speed <-1000-1000>
Sets the neighborhood directory to the path	<directory path>
Start sim logging	sim_log begin
End sim logging	sim_log end
Swap the two house files and updates families	swap_houses <house number> <house number>
Ticks disabled	sweep off
Ticks enabled	sweep on
Tile information displayed	tile_info on
Tile information hidden	tile_info off
Toggle camera mode	cam_mode
Toggle music	music
Toggle sound log window	sound_log
Toggle sounds	sound
Toggle web page creation	html
Total reload of people skeletons, animations, suits, and skins	reload_people
Trigger sound event	soundevent

CHAPTER 10:
EXTENDING YOUR WORLD

Introduction

Not that Maxis didn't pack *The Sims* with enough to do for months on end, but you can find additional tools, downloads, and links at the official website: *http://www.TheSims.com*. For the Sim hacker, the sky's the limit, thanks to an open game system that allows users to create and edit music and graphics files. The following sections give you a sneak peak at the free goodies awaiting you at the official *Sims* website.

Downloads

Art Studio!

Fig. 10-1. Click on the waving Sim for online help while using the program. Read the help windows, because the audio is in Sim-Speak.

This neat paint program lets you create original works of art for your Sims to buy, admire, and even sell. Your first step is to select a picture type (figure 10-2), which determines the size and style of painting.

Fig. 10-2. You can choose various sizes and designs for your picture, including a heart shape.

Next, you have the option to import any graphics file, regardless of size, as pictured in figure 10-3.

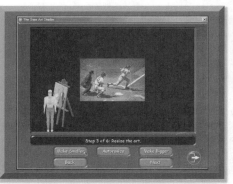

Fig. 10-3. We imported one of our favorite baseball pictures, then resized it to fit the painting window.

After selecting and sizing your picture, choose the texture and color of your frame, as pictured in figure 10-4.

Fig. 10-4. We opted for a rich walnut frame.

In the Catalog Info screen pictured here, set the price and enter a description of your new painting. Finally, save the painting. Choose a directory or use the default *UserObjects* subdirectory.

Fig. 10-5. After describing your painting and setting a price, save it to use in your game.

Sims File Cop

With all the files flying back and forth in the *Sims* community, you may inadvertently create or accept files that cause problems during a game session. The Sims File Cop examines your game directory for any damaged or risky files.

FaceLift

After playing *The Sims* for hours, you'll be ready for a few new faces in your neighborhood. After you register (no charge) at *The Sims* site, you can download FaceLift, a program that lets you create your own heads. You begin with a collection of nine randomly created heads, as pictured in figure 10-7. This is your starting point. If you don't see anything you like, click the Reset Faces button to create another set of nine.

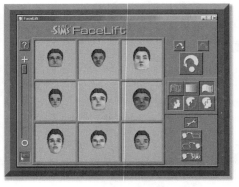

Fig. 10-7. Begin by choosing a head.

Use a combination of the Blend and Deform buttons, along with the Mutation Rate slider bar, to create variations of the face. Change the head and hair together, or work separately on each area. The changes are not seen immediately, but when you go back to the main screen, you can review the altered face.

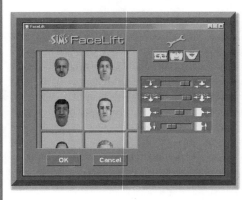

Fig. 10-8. The fine-tuning screen lets you change the size and shape of the nose, eyes, mouth, and jaw.

HomeCrafter

Fig. 10-9. HomeCrafter lets you view your creation in a Sims home setting.

This utility lets you design custom wallpapers and floors for your Sim houses. You create the patterns in any paint program, then use HomeCrafter to design the final product. If this sounds like too much work, check out one of the many *Sims* websites, such as *http://www.thesimsresource.com*, for thousands of user-created wallpapers (figure 10-10), floors (figure 10-11), and other items.

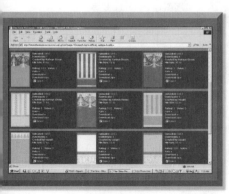

Fig. 10-10. Scroll through thousands of wallpaper designs and download your favorites.

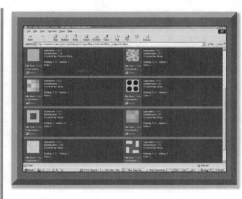

Fig. 10-11. More than 2,300 floors and counting!

SimShow

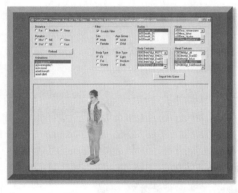

Fig. 10-12. SimShow lets you check out your skins before importing them into the game.

If you've always wanted to create yourself or your favorite celebrity to use in *The Sims*, the SimShow utility is a must-have. After creating or editing a skin using any paint program, SimShow lets you view a Sim skin from various angles. You can alter the skin using your libraries of bodies, heads, body textures, and head textures, then apply various game animations to see your creation in action. The utility also comes with a skin library, and of course, you can supplement it from the thousands of skins available at *TheSims.com* or several other *Sims* websites.

Objects, Skins, and Homes

The official *Sims* website can get you started with a variety of files for your game. This site (*thesims.com*) has a page of links to other great Sims sites, such as *thesimsresource.com*.

CAUTION

Remember to use File Cop to check the integrity of your **Sims** downloads.

NOTE

Most objects available on the website before **House Party** was released are included in **House Party**. Some are not included, however, like the new roses, the coming Potty Pack (porta-potties for **The Sims**), the trash pack, and the "Ukelele Lady Lamp."

Here are a few samples of what you can download from *TheSims.com*:

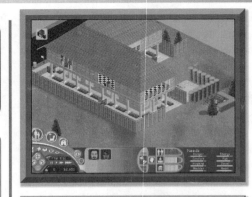

...and a reflecting pool around the perimeter.

Your Sims can play with their new guinea pig and enjoy a bouquet of red roses.

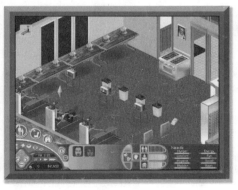

The Maximus house includes a workout room...

It's murder on a budget, but you'll find it hard to pass up a pull on the new slot machine.

...spa room with multiple showers...

What Sim party animal wouldn't love a new jukebox?

PART II:

The SiMs™
HOUSE PARTY
EXPANSION PACK

CHAPTER 11:
NEW TOYS

Introduction

House Party provides more than 50 new objects to fill your Sims' houses, all geared toward parties. In this chapter are complete tables listing every new item's purchase price, related Motives, and Efficiency ratings. As with the tables in the "Material Sims" chapter, you can use the information below to help you make informed decisions about what to buy to fulfill your Sims' needs within their budget.

If you're throwing parties in (or around) your Sims' home, you don't want it looking like a party palace all the time. Decorate on the day of your party; you can always sell back all the party supplies within 24 hours for a full refund. Long live money-back guarantees!

Fig. 11-1. This DJ booth earns a full refund if it's returned immediately after the party.

House Party Buying Guide

The following sections list the new *House Party* objects, broken down into a few logical subcategories to help you find what you're looking for quickly. These objects appear when you click the Buy Mode button on the control panel. We've added a few subcategories to make it easier to find a specific object. The Efficiency rating (1–10) is an indicator of how well the item satisfies each Motive, with a higher number being worth more to your Sims. The more expensive items offer better Motive satisfaction.

Seating

Chairs

Several new chairs have been added in *House Party*, encompassing all types (movable, stationary, and reclining). Most of the new seating fits into one of the party themes, although some items might find their way into some households' standard decor.

Freedom Chair

Type: Stationary

Cost: §65

Motive: Comfort (2)

Rusty Redneck Barrel Chair

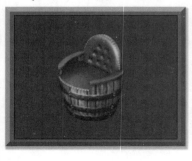

Type: Stationary

Cost: §100

Motive: Comfort (3)

nflatable Fun Chair

Type: Stationary

Cost: §109

Motives: Comfort (3), Room (1)

The Chair of the Future

Type: Movable

Cost: §203

Motive: Comfort (3)

Surplus Theatre Seating

Type: Stationary

Cost: §153

Motive: Comfort (3)

Tropi-Cane Island Chair

Type: Movable

Cost: §315

Motive: Comfort (5)

Tiki Dream Dining Chair

Type: Movable

Cost: §600

Motive: Comfort (3)

Cowch Country Lounger

Type: Stationary

Cost: §1,115

Motives: Comfort (8), Room (1)

Couches

A few new couches and loveseats complement the new themed chairs, rounding out your *House Party* seating options. Each of the three party themes has a corresponding loveseat or couch: A cow hair couch for country, a bamboo sofa for luaus, and an inflatable loveseat for your all-night raves. These seats don't offer your Sims dining places, but they can be a great place to stock up on Comfort in the midst of a party if you complement them with a television.

Inflatable Sofa (3 Colors)

Cost: §190

Motives: Comfort (3), Energy (5), Room (1)

Tropi-Cane Sofa

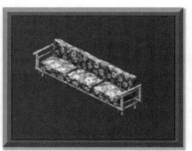

Cost: §535

Motives: Comfort (5), Energy (5)

Cowch Country Sofa

Cost: §1,350

Motives: Comfort (8), Energy (5), Room (1)

Surfaces

House Party comes with several new surfaces, only some of which are themed. Several new pieces may become staples of your standard households, as well, as they are tasteful and somewhat more conservative than the party-minded offerings. Surfaces are very important at parties, as your Sims will be looking for places to eat throughout the festivities.

TIP

The Efficiency Table is the answer to many a Sim player's dream: a one-square dining table. Now, Sim families of up to four can dine in style without taking up a 6 x 7 room! Likewise, the "Plus!" model gives you the game's only 1 x 2 dining table, making it an incredibly valuable addition for larger families with space concerns.

Countertops

Cape Crab Coastside Counter

Cost: §249

Country Counter

Cost: §276

End Tables

Freedom End Table

Cost: §40

ScienStone Wall Counter

Cost: §425

The Elegant Chef End Table

Cost: §50

The Smart Counter

Cost: §432

"Lola Mona" Occasional Table

Cost: §170

Desks/Tables

Efficiency Table

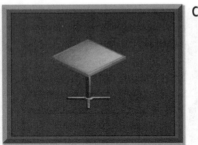

Cost: §179

Efficiency Table Plus!

Cost: §275

Artist's Concept Table

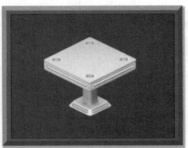

Cost: §349

Tiki Dream Dining Table

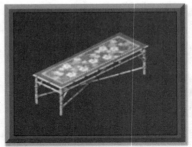

Cost: $379

Decorative

Of all the object categories, decorations contains the most new items in *House Party*. All the frills and ornaments you need to carry a party theme throughout your house are at your fingertips, from a set of mounted steer horns to a memorial surf board. These decorations are invaluable in upholding a maximum Room score for your party guests, which is one of the easiest ways to contribute to their overall mood (and thus your party score). Buy as many decorations as you can, and make sure all of the areas your party guests visit are chock-full of Room-raising objets d'art.

What a Gas! Party Balloons

Cost: §50

Motive: Room (3)

Notes: Party Balloons do attract visitors, but they pop gradually within a day, so they aren't a good long-term decorating investment.

Desert Nut Lawn Ornament

Cost: §70

Motive: Room (1)

"Amaizing" Lawn Ornament

Cost: §89

Motive: Room (2)

Jungle Jumble Import Display

Cost: §151

Motive: Room (1)

Pacific Island Relic

Cost: §198

Motive: Room (2)

"Duke Tubula" Memorial Surf Board

Cost: §230

Motive: Room (2)

Scraps Ranch Rag Rug

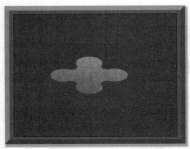

Cost: §233

Motive: Room (2)

Beaver Pelt Moosehead

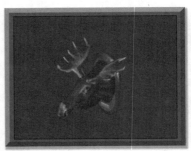

Cost: §450

Motive: Room (2)

Davant-Naif Art Rug

Cost: §290

Motive: Room (2)

Weft Wrights Wall Quilt

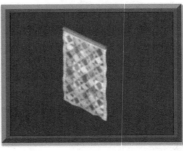

Cost: §515

Motive: Room (2)

Long Horn Wall Accent

Cost: §395

Motive: Room (3)

"Black Bile Bear"

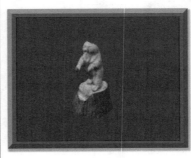

Cost: §520

Motive: Room (3)

"Native Sim Wall Hanging"

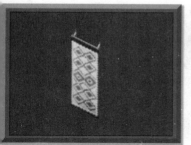

Cost: §639

Motives: Room (3)

SimBad's Stuffed Marlin

Cost: §777

Motive: Room (3)

"Blue Inca Pilot" Band Poster

Cost: §1,789

Motive: Room (4)

Ali'i Kahuna Ceremonial Tiki

Cost: §2,000

Motive: Room (5)

Electronics

TIP

Party electronics are another great candidate for immediate store return after your Sims have partied hard with them. Buy your party gadgets right before your big bash, then send them back to the store immediately after the party for a full refund. You'll be sighing with relief when all §7,129 goes back into your bank account when you return that DJ Booth!

Dance Aids

No dancing experience is complete without some hip and fly electronic dance devices! These dancing accessories are sure to please your party guests when coupled with a stereo. Place them close to some speakers so your Sims can get the benefits of the dance aid and the music at the same time.

TIP

The dance floor in combination with a stereo is the most important ingredient for any party. The flashing lights add to the fun of a dancing experience, and because dancing is an activity you can direct guest Sims to partake in, it's one of the best ways to manage your party mood.

"Bounce My Booty" Dance Floor

Cost: §1,250

Motives: Fun (6), Room (2)

Spazmatronic Plasmatronic Go-Go Cage

Cost: §1,749

Motives: Fun (7), Room (3)

Notes: These cages are a great themed addition to a dance floor, plus they can be a group activity because Sims can watch the dancer.

Musical Equipment

Sound systems make up much of the new electronics suite in the expansion pack. From a professional-grade disc jockey booth to an authentic mechanical bull, these gadgets are the backbones of a successful party. Sport at least a few of them at any bash you host.

Neukum Stereo Speakers

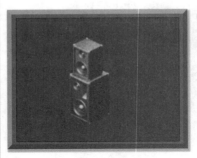

Cost: §99

Motive: Room (1)

Notes: Neukums provide excellent satellite speakers for your DJ booth, allowing you to cover large rooms or even multiple rooms.

Turntablitz DJ Booth

Cost: §7,129

Motives: Fun (8), Room (3)

Notes: Group activity. The DJ Booth is the ultimate sound system, with an option for Playful Sims to DJ or even turn up the funk with a little scratch. Technically, you could even use this as your home stereo system if your Sims are serious audiophiles.

ToroTec Mechanical Bull

Cost: §5,678

Motive: Fun (4)

Skill: Body

Notes: Group activity. The optimal difficulty setting depends on your Sim's Body Skill: Select higher difficulty levels for a fit Sim to get maximum payoff. While you're on the bull, coax guests to watch your Sim ride, adding to their Fun.

Plumbing

There are a few new plumbing items in the expansion, although only one of them has anything to do with party themes. Besides being a luau-themed object, you'll also find the Wicked Breeze Surf Shower is a viable alternative to the SpaceMiser Shower. Although it provides one less Hygiene point per use, it does add to your Room score, which can be notoriously low in cramped bathrooms.

Boggs Memorial Commode

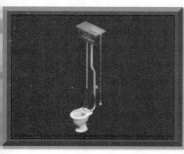

Cost: §375

Motive: Bladder (8)

Chrome Faucet System

Cost: §622

Motive: Hygiene (3)

Wicked Breeze Surf Shower

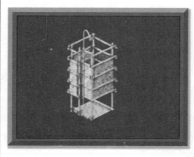

Cost: §672

Motives: Hygiene (5), Room (1)

Lighting

There are several party-themed lights in your expanded Buy Screen lists, including additional wall lights, which were not included in the original release of The Sims. Check out the Club Code Thrill Light stacks if you're looking for some serious partying—coupled with a dance floor and a DJ booth, these turn any house into Party Central.

TIP

Especially with big ticket items such as the dance club lights, return your party purchases immediately after the guests go home. You'll enjoy their use without having to pay a dime, and they are fairly inconvenient (and unsightly) to store.

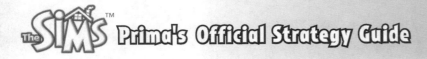

Floor Lamps

Faux Blowfish Fish Lamp

Cost: §173

Motive: None

Old Railroad Lamp

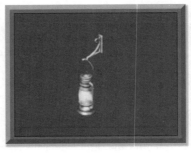

Cost: §63

Motive: None

Club Code Thrill Light

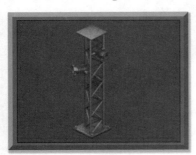

Cost: §1,000

Motive: Room (1)

LED Pod Light

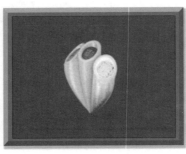

Cost: §131

Motive: None

Wall Lamps

SUNOT Shop Light

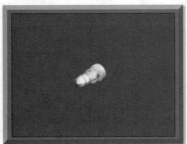

Cost: §30

Motive: None

Symbol Light

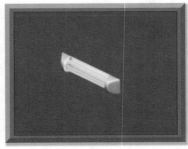

Cost: §135

Motive: None

Miscellaneous

Several new party objects fall under the general header of "miscellaneous items." Along with the traditional objects such as bookcases and bars, you'll also find things that are specifically geared toward getting down. Many of these items bear a little explanation, so there are usage notes under some of the more exotic entries.

Bookshelves

Ornery Owl Pioneer Bookcase

Cost: §935

Motive: Fun (3)

Skills: Cooking, Mechanical, Study

Galvanator Bookshelf

Cost: §925

Motive: Fun (3)

Skills: Cooking, Mechanical, Study

Bars

Whether Vain Drink Dispenser

Cost: §920

Motives: Hunger (1), Fun (3), Room (3)

Antique Saloon Drink Cabinet

Cost: §922

Motives: Hunger (1), Fun (3), Room (3)

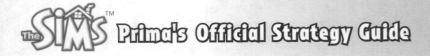

Party Accessories

Punchucopia Extraordinaria

Cost: §150

Motives: Hunger (1), Fun (2)

Notes: Group activity. The punch bowl encourages social interactions—just like the water cooler at work. Place the punch bowl atop a surface, and the Elegant Chef End Table makes an excellent choice.

The Elegant Chef Buffet Table

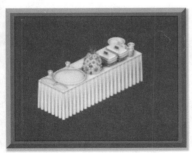

Cost: §194

Motive: Hunger (4)

Notes: Group activity. You'll have to pay an additional §350 to hire a Caterer, unless you want your Sims to stock this table themselves (which you don't). Make the Caterer as essential a part of any party, as the food he serves up!

Fancy Feet Cake Treat

Cost: §300

Motive: Fun (3)

Notes: Group activity. Put this in an open area, then have one of your Sims use it to hire an entertainer when the time is right. There is no additional cost to hire the dancer; purchasing the cake pays the fee.

KampRite Instant Campfire

Cost: §482

Motives: Comfort (2), Fun (2)

Notes: Group activity. If a Sim with a Charisma Skill rating of six or better chooses Tell Story, there is a 1 in 10 chance of a haunting by the Campfire Ghost.

Porta-Parody Costume Trunk

Cost: §496

Motive: None

Notes: Group activity. By choosing one of the themes from the trunk's pie menu, everyone at the party will change into an outfit that matches the selected theme.

"Bezique's Folly" Card Game

Cost: §502

Motive: Fun (2)

Skill: Charisma

Notes: Group activity. This version of Charades entertains several people at a time, but its usefulness is eclipsed by any of the other party items.

Super Schlooper Bubble Blower

Cost: §710

Motive: Comfort (2), Fun (3)

Notes: Group activity. This object provides your Sims with a giggle fest that can be shared by up to four at a time.

Object Advertising Table

Just like the original *Sims*, the *House Party* game objects advertise their ability to satisfy your Sims' needs. The following table lists each new object alphabetically, and shows the interactions possible with that object. It also shows which Motives are fulfilled by each interaction, and how many points each interaction advertises. Also listed are any Sim personality traits that increase the perceived value of certain objects, and finally the degree to which the appeal of each item drops off over increasing distance.

OBJECT TYPE	POSSIBLE INTERACTIONS	MOTIVE ADVERTISED	ADVERTISED VALUE	PERSONALITY TRAIT MODIFIER	REDUCED EFFECTS (OVER DISTANCE)
Bar	Have a Drink	Room	30	N/A	Low
"Bezique's Folly" Card Game	Play	Fun	42	Outgoing	High
	Join	Fun	40	N/A	High
	Join	Social	60	N/A	High
Bookshelf	Read a Book	Fun	30	Serious	High
"Bounce My Booty" Dance Floor	Dance	Fun	60	Active	High
	Join	Social	70	N/A	High
	Join	Fun	55	N/A	High
Chair (Stationary)	Sit	Comfort	20	N/A	Medium
Chair (Movable)	Sit	Comfort	25	N/A	Medium
Decoration (Marlin)	View	Fun	7	N/A	High
Decoration (All Others)	View	Fun	5	N/A	High
Elegant Chef Buffet Table	Grab a Plate	Hunger	95	N/A	Low
	Clean	Room	40	Neat	High
Fancy Feet Cake Treat (Exotic Dancer)	Watch	Social	50	Playful	High
	Clean Up	Room	40	Neat	High
KampRite Instant Campfire	Sit	Fun	42	Charisma	Medium
	Join	Fun	42	N/A	Medium
	Join	Social	60	N/A	Medium
Punchucopia Extraordinaria	Drink	Comfort	50	N/A	Medium
	Drink	Hunger	70	N/A	Medium
Shower	Clean	Room	20	Neat	High
	Take a Shower	Hygiene	50	Neat	Medium
Sink	Wash Hands	Hygiene	10	Neat	High
Sofa/Loveseat	Nap	Energy	40	Lazy	High
	—	Comfort	5	Lazy	High
	Sit	Comfort	30	Lazy	Medium

OBJECT TYPE	POSSIBLE INTERACTIONS	MOTIVE ADVERTISED	ADVERTISED VALUE	PERSONALITY TRAIT MODIFIER	REDUCED EFFECTS (OVER DISTANCE)
Spazmatronic Plasmatronic Go-Go Cage	Dance	Fun	61	Outgoing	High
	Watch	Fun, Social	40	N/A	High
Super Schlooper Bubble Blower	Blow Bubbles	Fun	45	Creativity, Playful	High
	Join	Fun	45	N/A	Low
	Join	Social	65	N/A	High
Toilet	Clean (Both Toilets)	Room	40	Neat	High
	Flush (Hygeia-O-Matic)	Room	30	Neat	High
	Unclog (Both Toilets)	Room	50	Neat	High
	Use (Hygeia-O-Matic)	Bladder	50	N/A	Low
	— (Flush Force)	Bladder	70	N/A	Low
ToroTec Mechanical Bull	Ride	Fun	45	Active	Medium
	Watch	Social	40	N/A	High
Turntablitz DJ Booth	Turn Off	Energy	220	Neat	Medium
	Turn On	Fun	30	Playful	High
	Dance	Fun	40	Outgoing	High
	DJ	Fun	65	Creativity	High
	Watch	Fun	40	Shy	High

CHAPTER 12:
SIM PARTY ANIMALS

Introduction

You'll find several new Non-Player Characters (NPCs) in the game. With everything from a flirtatious Caterer to a fireside apparition, *House Party* adds a wealth of potential interactions to your Sims' lives. If your party gets epic, you may get some interesting characters to show up! This chapter introduces you to these new characters, with explanations of who they are, what they do, and how to find (or avoid) them.

The Campfire Ghost

House Party includes a new Campfire object, which can only be placed outside. The Campfire is one of the simplest means of getting large groups of Sims to interact and have fun while they're at it. To get the Ghost to show up, gather a group around the fire and start telling stories. Your storyteller must be an adult Sim with a Charisma Skill of six or higher. Each time a qualifying Sim selects Tell Story from the Campfire pie menu, the Ghost has a 1 in 10 chance of showing up in the shadows. It's a rare sighting, but it's a ton of fun to watch the Campfire Ghost haunt your Sims!

Fig. 12-1. The Campfire promotes Social interaction and Fun, and it's an inexpensive purchase to boot!

Party Services

To really get your walls shaking, you need some hired help. Two NPCs are available for your Sims to shell out their hard-earned Simoleans to, and both are essential to a proper house party. Both also have item requirements, meaning you have to purchase objects using Buy Mode to get full use from your party personnel. When the party is winding down, dismiss your hired help by clicking on them and selecting "Dismiss."

Caterer

The Caterer is the first person you should think about when prepping for your party. This sociable chef will keep any buffet tables and punch bowls you have laid out filled to the brim, freeing your Sims up to get down to the business of partying. If he runs out of things to do, he'll start hitting on your guests, and when he swings he usually misses!

Fig. 12-2. The Caterer is a pretty sociable, so keep him busy or he'll busy himself with your guests!

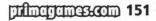

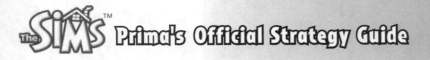

Hire the Caterer over the phone, under the Services pie menu. He costs §350 for one 24-hour period, so unless you are planning to have a multi-day rave (and you'll lose people to sleep long before that), the Caterer is pretty much a one-price proposition. To make any use of his services, you need to purchase at least one Buffet Table. He'll cover multiple tables if you think you need it (if you have more than one party room, for example). You can also purchase a Buffet End Table to accommodate a Punch bowl. Punch bowls are great for parties—as people partake of the punch, you'll find that they become more sociable.

Fig. 12-3. Entertainers have a knack for sweeping your guests off their feet!

If you see the Caterer wandering too far from his position, have one of your Sims tell him to get back to work! He can be detrimental to your Party Score, as most of the people he bothers don't appreciate his attentions.

Entertainer

The Entertainer is sure to please your Sims and is an easy way to boost the Mood. Sim children won't find much of interest in a dancer's lewd gyrations, but both sexes of adult Sims will be highly entertained no matter what gender of dancer you hire. Just lay down the cash and watch your Mood Moose antlers perk up! Let the Entertainers stick around the party after their show, because they do the secondary job of perking up your guests via conversation and special interactions such as the one shown in figure 12-3.

To hire an Entertainer, you need to buy a Fancy Feet Cake Treat. Place it facing an open area to allow your Sims plenty of space from which to view the show. When you're ready, have an adult use the cake, and select Hire Male Dancer or Hire Female Dancer, as you desire. As soon as you've done so, most of the partygoers will stop whatever they're doing and gather to enjoy the show. When your dancer is finished, someone must dispose of the cake, as it is not reusable.

The Partiers

As your party progresses, you may get some uninvited guests. Which one you get depends on the relative success of your party: a dud will draw the kooky Psycho Mime, while a truly legendary rager will attract a suprising guest! Chapter 15, "Let's Party" explains how to manage your party score so the coolest guest shows up every time. If you happen to attract one of these characters, keep your eye on them—their antics are very entertaining.

Psycho Mime

If a freaky mute with a pale face shows up at your doorstep, you've attracted the Psycho Mime. Entertaining though he may be, if he's around, the chances are your party isn't exactly up to snuff. He only comes by if your party's mood is less than 15, and he stays around until it perks up above 25. The Psycho Mime is the only partier who shows up at an all-family party (which is at least five family members plus the Caterer). Furthermore, your party must be at least 90 minutes old before the Psycho Mime has a chance of showing up.

The Mime is also a kleptomaniac. He swipes food from the buffet table and any small things left on a table or counter. The only thing he'll steal that isn't on the countertop is the Bezique's Folly set, to practice with at home.

> ### TIP
>
> *The Psycho Mime helps your party's mood, thanks to his entertaining antics. Therefore, even though he is an indicator that your party is a bit of a downer, it's better to keep him on*

Party Crashers

Party Crashers are random freeloaders who can come in and join your party. Although they are strangers, they are generally well behaved, so you don't have to worry about losing any of your belongings. You can ask them to leave, though you may be told to get lost. In fact, Party Crashers can actually help your party score, as they generally come ready to have a good time. However, if you see them disturbing any of your invited guests, it's time to ask them to leave (see figure 12-4).

Fig. 12-4. If you're lucky, you can get a Party Crasher to hit the road just by asking.

Party Crashers show up once your party is at least 120 game-minutes old. The party score has to be at 40 or higher, which means that you'll need several guests, and most of them have to be pretty happy to be there. Party Crashers won't always leave when asked, but because they are only there for your party, they find their way home (or to the next party) when your party ends. But be careful, Party Crashers will sometimes sleep over.

Secret Celebrity

A mystery guest can grace your party if your shindig is swingin' enough. Your party score must be above 55, and your party has to be at least 135 minutes old for word of your rave to reach the celebrity guest. Given the obligations of fame, the celebrity will only stay for a maximum of four hours. If your party ends before then, the mystery guest will leave when you send your other guests home. Also, the celebrity will call it quits on your party if your party score drops below 45, so be sure to keep your people happy if you want to keep the star around.

CHAPTER 13:
SETTING THE MOOD

Introduction

This chapter will help you create the proper atmosphere for a successful party. For your fickle Sims to get in the mood for an all-nighter, they've got to have all the ingredients for fun at their fingertips. From party objects to house planning and decor, the following sections contain everything you need to boogie down 'til the cows come home (or at least until the cops shut you down).

A Place to Party

The new walls, floors, doors, and other construction objects included in *House Party* will tempt you to create a purpose-built party palace, with every party object in the game laid out for your Sims' hedonistic delights. However, your most successful parties will be held in well-developed homes that are primarily single-family residences and have simply been designed with entertaining in mind. While you can certainly construct dazzling nightclubs such as the Fun Factory shown in figure 13-1, you might find it harder to achieve your highest party scores in these buildings.

Fig. 13-1. The Fun Factory was designed to be a dedicated party paradise, complete with every party object in the game.

Building for Success

If you plan on throwing parties, concentrate on building a strong, well-planned house that focuses first on satisfying the needs of your residents. A solid single-family home is best for hosting parties because it ensures that the residents themselves will be happy and successful, with a solid network of friends. Not only is it important for your hosts to be in a good mood themselves, they also need to have an income to support their party habits! Since dedicated party pads focus on maximizing party activities and decor, they aren't as efficient at keeping Sims happy on a day-to-day basis.

A proper party house is little different than a house you would build for any Sim family. You need a good, straightforward layout, high quality objects for keeping your Sims happy, and coverage of all their basic needs. As you build your house, simply keep a place in mind for entertaining, be it an extra-large living room, a dedicated party space such as a "garage," or even a backyard patio with a hot tub and plenty of open space.

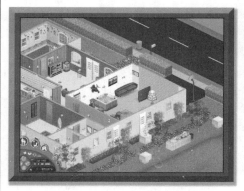

Fig. 13-2. This home features a "garage" dedicated to partying, as well as ample space for dancing and dipping out on the back deck.

Sharing Your Space

Party homes do have a few other considerations for the budding architect, but really they apply to all homes, as well. Because your house will be hosting a large number of Sims at one time, it's important not to build any bottlenecks in your routes through the home. Make all of your hallways two squares wide, so that your Sims and guests can pass each other in the hall. As a matter of fact, try to make *all* passages in the hall two squares wide. Use double doors in all major exits from the home, and leave two squares between household objects in major traffic lanes as shown in figure 13-3.

Fig. 13-3. Not all rooms need to be established with doors and walls—feel free to let some of your interior spaces flow into each other with open pathways.

You also need to bear the needs of your guests in mind while they are in your Sims' home. Between the Caterer's creations and the punch bowl, your guests will be showing red in the Bladder department pretty often, and these impatient Sims don't bother to form lines! Include up to twice as many bathrooms in a party house as you would if you were just building for your own Sims, to avoid backups in your bathrooms. Don't be afraid to construct half baths, either, which have only a sink and a toilet. Your guests won't be bathing at your house, so just the bare essentials are required to relieve them in their times of need.

Happy Pathing

Even one confusing switchback in your home can leave Sims feeling like lab rats trapped in a maze. Often, the only solution is to walk them out through a succession of Go Here commands, which is both tedious and time consuming, distracting you and your Sim from the business of finding happiness. Make sure you don't build any areas in your home that have only one exit and include a bend or turn.

Fig. 13-4. Small corridors get your Sims into foot-traffic jams all the time, wasting your time and effort untying the logic knots they get themselves into.

Remember that this situation isn't just limited to wall placement—objects sitting on your floor can also create constricted pathways that befuddle your simple Sims. Whenever a traffic lane bends, make sure you have at least a two-square width along its entire length. Single-square passages are sure to confuse your Sims even if they have multiple exits, so stay away from creating these cramped quarters whenever you expect Sims to go *through* an area.

The Fun Factory

Even though it's harder to throw the mother of all parties in a purpose-built party house, the new themed textures and objects in *House Party* are too tempting to pass up. The "Fun Factory" was built as a nightclub stocked with all the latest and greatest attractions in the party world, right up to the trendy oxygen bars and seductive dance cages. The following section shows off some of the Fun Factory's features, which you can use to fuel your own nightclub ideas.

Fig. 13-5. The exterior of the Fun Factory is made to resemble a remodeled machine shop, so the textures are all slanted toward the industrial.

The Entrance

The Fun Factory is a converted machine shop based upon an industrial theme. To this end, we used a brick exterior wallpaper with the industrial salvage windows, the sheet metal doors, and even threw in a few industrial fans for effect. The new velvet ropes line the entrance, providing crowd control for our special invite-only events.

> ### TIP
>
> *Some decor decisions are based upon form instead of function. The bar near the entrance and the narrow bathrooms with stalls are just two examples of this. Were you to build a place for party score instead of for looks, you'd want to stick with a normal house as covered above under "Building for Success."*

The main entry consists of double doors, helping to keep traffic flowing (hopefully all flowing *in*). Upon entry, guests immediately find themselves on the dance floor, complete with a DJ booth, lighted dance pads, and dance cages on all four corners. To the right, an oxygen bar serves up refreshments of all kinds. Above the bar hangs examples of all the neon signs available in the game (some of which are considered lights, while others are grouped with decorations).

Fig. 13-6. The front of our party palace is decked out with the very best in dance floor decor.

The Courtyard

The Fun Factory is centered on an open courtyard in the middle of the building, which sports a hot tub and pool. Because you cannot designate open-roofed spaces inside the outer walls of your structures in *The Sims*, we've left a small passageway open to the outside, visible in the lower right of figure 13-7. By keeping this small passage to the outside open, all the windows lining the pool area effectively deliver light to the interior spaces, greatly increasing the ambient light levels in our building during the day. To prevent party crashers and other undesirables from sneaking in through this passageway, we've blocked it off with hedges.

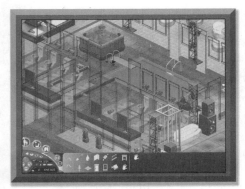

Fig. 13-7. A narrow corridor linking the interior courtyard to the outside walls keeps the central area open to the world, greatly adding to the room values in the main body of the building.

Flanking the exterior hallway are separate restrooms for men and women. Your Sims will even respect the gender designations, plus, the doors are still a great way to add character to your party shack. The new hanging counters complete with sinks and vanity mirrors complete the bath area, and concessions to Sim pathing limitations are made in the form of multiple doors leading into the bathrooms.

Opposite the bathrooms is a large, themed dining area. Nothing says "party" like inflatable furniture, and this room has more than its fair share. You could feed a whole squad of Marines in here! (Go on, try it—get everyone in the neighborhood started in Military careers, and then invite them all over for a bash!) Cluttered though the room may seem, it has a two-square pathway along its entire length from front to back, and the chairs are arranged to allow passage to the rear rows no matter how many guests are sitting at the front tables. Large plate glass windows line the wall facing the courtyard, providing diners with unrestricted views of the scantily-clad Sims in the water.

The Rodeo and the Residence

The rear of the building is the only two-story area on the property. The whole back end of the building is a single, large, open space filled with caterer's tables, inflatable sofas, and various party objects. The centerpiece is the mechanical bull, which can be seen from the pool deck through the gigantic loft-style window. In the back corner is a teleporter that leads up to the second floor, which contains a Spartan living area (after all, someone has to live here to invite everyone over).

Fig. 13-8. The Rodeo Room even hosts a costume trunk for theme nights at the Fun Factory.

Decorating for Your Party

The *House Party* expansion pack includes more than 50 new objects for your partying pleasure, plus new textures for decorating. Unless you are building a themed building such as the Fun Factory, you'll want to spiff up your residence on the day of the party to get your party groove on.

Equipment Rental

When you are ready to host a party, wait to purchase your party objects until just before you're ready to bring down the house. Most homes don't lend themselves to DJ booths, dance cages, mechanical bulls, or nightclub light racks as permanent decor! Because the game allows you to sell new items back to the stores within 24 hours without depreciation, you can essentially "rent" your party items for free if you hold onto them for less than a day. The only exception to this is the Fancy Feet Cake Treat, which is reduced to trash once it has been used.

First, secure a DJ booth and a little room for dancing on an electronic dance floor. A few dance cages are the perfect complement to any dance floor, and your special event lighting needs can be covered with the disco light stacks. Music is a staple of any party—Sims with nothing else to do will often occupy their time by dancing, which increases their Fun and generally improves the mood of the party.

> **TIP**
>
> *Not all Sims like the same music. If you've got a Sim to spare for the DJ booth, pay attention to what music keeps your Sims dancing the longest, and stick with it for best results on the Mood Moose.*

Fig. 13-9. A dance floor is the foundation of a good party.

A hot tub is an essential part of any party. Even though this item is not new with the *House Party* expansion, it is the key to the longevity of a good bash. Sims can increase their valuable Comfort and Hygiene levels in the bubbling water, which have no other real aids at a party. Most of a Sim's time is spent standing up at a party, which quickly diminishes their Comfort level. Furthermore, the activity is Fun, and provides Social interaction to boot, which puts it ahead of sitting on some boring sofa to soak up the Comfort.

Food is another key to the success of a good get-together. Although the Caterer is a bit pricey, he is one of the basic building blocks of a proper party. Place a buffet table and a punch bowl in an open area with lots of access. Don't forget to locate a few tables and plenty of chairs nearby, or your guests will eat on their feet, costing them precious Comfort and Energy as they stuff their faces. Even if you're having a relatively small party, have the Caterer on hand both to cover your nutritional needs and to help qualify the party as an official event with the game (see Chapter 15 for more on that topic).

> **TIP**
>
> *Plan your party to focus on one primary area in your home. The more you concentrate your guests, the more likely they are to mingle and participate in group activities. If you spread them out across the property, they'll waste time and energy finding each other at the party.*

Next, plan your group activity objects. Will you be blowing bubbles all night long, laughing hysterically as an Entertainer steps out of a cake? Is dancing the focus of your party? Maybe you're inviting Mr. and Mrs. StuffySim over for the evening, and so a nice parlor game is more your speed. You could even go for a nice campfire out in the backyard. Don't be afraid to purchase multiple objects to entertain your guests. After all, you've got to keep them entertained over an extended period of time, and they won't all have the same interests.

Party Themes

The *House Party* expansion pack features a wide assortment of options for adding themed decor to your home. Walls, floors, doorways, and even furniture come in several new variations that can combine to make one of three special party themes: Western, Luau, or Rave. You can bring the special objects in for the duration of your party, or you can go so far as to redecorate your entire house with one of the new themes.

Not only are there new themes for your rooms, but you can also acquire matching outfits for your Sims! The best way to get your Sims dressed to party is to provide them with a costume trunk, and place it within easy access. Direct your Sims to use the chest, and your guests will follow their lead. In addition to the three room themes, there are also Roman and Medieval outfits to help your Sims fit into the theme of your party.

Fig. 13-10. Sim-Hawaii! The additional themed items allow you to create your own themed parties, rooms, or even houses.

CHAPTER 14:
HOUSE PARTY
NEIGHBORHOODS

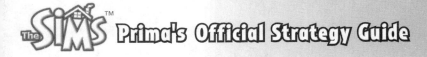

Introduction

House Party adds three entire neighborhoods to your *Sims* game, each with 10 additional lots to accommodate your block parties. These new neighborhoods are in addition to the four added by the *Livin' Large* expansion, giving you a grand total of 8 neighborhoods with both expansions installed, for your suburban sprawling pleasure. This chapter will help you make the most of your multiple neighborhoods, manage families, and import houses like the land-developing mogul you were born to be!

Neighborhood Management

Access to your additional neighborhoods in *House Party* is only a click away in the Neighborhood screen (see figure 14-1). To switch between your neighborhoods, click on the left or right arrows in the screen's upper left. You can manually add up to 99 neighborhoods. Simply make a copy of the *TemplateUserData* folder in your *The Sims* directory, and then rename it to *UserData##*, where ## is any unused number between 9 and 99. You can see which numbers you've used already by looking in the directory.

Fig. 14-1. The Neighborhood screen provides you with access to your additional Sim subdivisions.

Each neighborhood is essentially a separate universe; you can't make friends with Sims from a different neighborhood, and you won't see folks from the next subdivision strolling down your sidewalk. Furthermore, time stands still in the other neighborhoods while you play in one, so don't worry about having to manage every family you've created in multiple neighborhoods. While you can technically switch to any family in any neighborhood at any time, you may find it easier to focus on one neighborhood at a time, investing in the families and relationships there before moving on to the next neighborhood of Sims.

CAUTION

*If you install the **Livin' Large** expansion after **House Party**, you will lose all of your data in neighborhoods 2–5, so be sure to check the readme.txt file included on the **House Party** CD.*

Additional neighborhoods are a great way to try out different combinations of families, or even different flavors of games. For example, you may take one of your neighborhoods seriously, and focus your families on career advancement, home improvement, and growth. Perhaps you might devote another neighborhood to theme houses, with a '60's family, a gothic family, a ramshackle family, etc. Because the neighborhoods are completely separate from each other, you can go as wild as you want in a given neighborhood without affecting the integrity of your other neighborhoods.

Juggling Families

One of the most intriguing features of *The Sims* is the ability to share families with other players via the Internet. By publishing your families on *www.thesims.com*, you can allow people all over the world to share your little creations. Conversely, there are a multitude of families available online that other players have uploaded, and you can easily import these families into your own neighborhoods.

Fig. 14-2. Importing families is easy once you get the hang of it!

TIP

*Start your search for new families and houses at **www.thesims.com**. Not only will you find new families and homes here, but you'll also find links to many other Sims sites with their own offerings.*

When you're shopping for families online, note that families and houses are lot-specific. This means that you cannot select which lot an imported family inhabits in your neighborhood; it must be inserted into the lot it was designed for. If that lot is not available in your neighborhood but you want to use the family anyway, either replace the existing family with the new one, or import the new family into a different neighborhood.

When you find a family online that you'd like to bring into one of your neighborhoods, simply download it into your *The Sims\UserData\Import* folder. By default, this is on your C drive under *Program Files\Maxis*. After you've saved the family to your computer, run *The Sims*. Using the neighborhood selection arrows, switch to the neighborhood you want to import the family to. Then, click on the Import Family button (it looks like a house with a plus sign next to it) on the top center of the Neighborhood screen. This brings up the dialogue box pictured in figure 14-2. Select the family you want to import, and you'll immediately have a new family in town!

CHAPTER 15:
LET'S PARTY!

Introduction

You've saved up some cash, made some friends in the neighborhood, bought a slew of party goods, and decked out your Sims' house to perfection. You're ready to party! Now what? This chapter will help you get your party started. More importantly, once the entire population of your neighborhood is hanging out in your living room looking to you for entertainment, the following information will help you keep the party going strong into the wee hours of the morning.

Preparations

If you haven't checked it out already, this would be a good time to review pre-party preparations in the "Setting the Mood" chapter. By now, you probably have a house fit for entertaining, and you know how to stock it with all the party-ware and party-wear you need for an epic event. On the big day, have your Sims skip work so they can take care of their personal needs. Spoil them all morning. Have your Sim with the highest Cooking Skill serve up a little breakfast. While the meal is being prepared, you can send your other Sims to the bathroom, or perhaps enjoy a few moments in front of the television.

After you feed your Sims, have them engage in some sort of group fun activity. TV does the trick, especially if you've got a comfortable sofa they can sit on together. A Bubble Blower can also give your Sims a quick boost on the Fun bar, plus their Comfort will increase at the same time. When your Sims have had a good time, send as many of them as you can off to the bath. If you have more Sims than you have bathtubs, have the others attend to whatever need is most pressing while the others bathe.

Just after noon, have all of your Sims settle in for a nice long nap, to rest up for the long night ahead. As your Sims slumber, buy all of your party objects: dance floors, a DJ booth, temporary lighting—anything you want to use at the party. Wake your Sims up at about 4 p.m., a little before most Sims get home from work. Take care of any urgent needs they have, and then call the Caterer via the Services menu on the telephone. Hiring a Caterer is the true beginning of a party.

Fig. 15-2. Once you've hired the Caterer, the party is on!

Fig. 15-1. Our resident Cooking expert prepares a meal while the other Sims relax on the morning of their party.

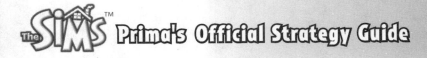

As soon as you're off the phone with the Caterer, start your invite calls by selecting Throw Party from the Phone menu. Pause after one invitation for the first hour or so of game time. Each time you make a call, you're inviting five random people over. Five should do it for now. Some Sims aren't home from work yet, and the others will serve you better later in the party if they are relatively "fresh."

Parties are much more likely to be successful for established host families with strong Relationships with the other Sims in the neighborhood. Social interactions generally go better between Sims when they are friends, and parties are all about socializing!

Fig. 15-3. The first party guests have arrived!

How the Game Scores Your Party

Once your party has begun, you have one goal: keep everyone happy. As soon as you have five Sims in the house plus the Caterer, the game activates something that tells it a party is underway. These five Sims may be any combination of residents or guests, but your party can never attract NPCs other than the Psycho Mime without at least five nonresident guests at the party.

Unlike standard social calls, you don't have to greet your party guests at the door. The first couple of guests will ring the doorbell, but then immediately make their way to the happenings on their own, freeing your hosts up to keep the party going!

The game determines a party score based upon the average overall Mood of all the Sims in attendance, plus other factors (like the number of guests). The overall Mood ranges from +100 (every Sim at the party having a maxed Mood bar) to −100 (full red bars on every Sim's Mood bar). The moosehead trophy (aka Mood Moose) indicates your party's overall Mood only. The antlers drooping shows that the Mood is poor. The antlers will be at full extension and will clearly project above the top of the mounting plaque when the mood is the highest. The Mood Moose does *not* determine the party score, but it can help you determine the Mood, which leads to a higher party score.

Fig. 15-4. The antlers on the Mood Moose give you a general sense of how well your party is going. Usually, you see them at half height.

After about 90 minutes of game time, your party qualifies for a possible appearance by the Psycho Mime. If by that time your party score is at 15 or less, he'll show up and start up his strange antics. The Psycho Mime will even come to parties that don't have any invited guests, as long as there are at least five residents and a Caterer in the house (with enough guests, the Caterer is not necessary). The other party NPCs require at least five guests at the party who do not live at the house.

After 120 game minutes of partying, Party Crashers can show up if your party score is at 40 or higher. These Sims do not live in the neighborhood, and any interactions your neighborhood Sims have will not help them in any permanent way. One of the best reasons to have a party is to help the entire neighborhood improve Relationships between Sims, perhaps even forming new friendships. Party Crashers detract from that effort somewhat, although they help your overall party score by counting as an additional guest. It's up to you to decide whether it is more important to keep your party score up, or invest in the long-term Relationships in the neighborhood.

Fig. 15-5. Party Crashers are a sign that your guests are enjoying themselves, so their appearance is always welcome (even if their **continued** presence is not).

Fleeting Fun

Your party is considered to be active until your total number of nonservice Sims on the property drops below five. As long as the party is still going on, the game causes your Sims to drop their Fun bars by two points every five game minutes, in addition to the normal rate of decay. This accelerated boredom is enforced on each Sim until his or her Fun rating drops to 0 (which is halfway), at which time the Fun reverts to a normal rate of decay. If the Sim rejuvenates his or her Fun bar, the game kicks in to enforce enjoyment mediocrity again.

Party Scoring

The game keeps track of the score, and tallies it every 20 game minutes to determine what NPCs are going to show up at the party. In addition to the average mood of the partygoers, the game also adds two points for every guest at the party. The more guests you have, the harder it is to manage their moods. However, multiple guests mean a higher party score. It's up to you to decide what's better: an easier-to-manage party, or higher attendance for more bonus points.

Fig. 15-6. More guests mean more to manage for the host, but at +2 party score per head, additional guests definitely earn their keep.

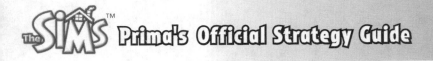

Keeping the Party Going

After the first 60 minutes of game time, start inviting more guests. If you invite everyone over early, they will be too tired to participate in your party in the all-important third hour, when your score is evaluated for attracting Party Crashers. As soon as your new guests arrive, hire an Entertainer, and watch the crowds gather in front of the cake. Your new guests should immediately be drawn to the party area, which will help boost their mood (thereby increasing your overall party score).

Fig. 15-7. If one of your guests got up on the wrong side of the bed this morning, send him packing; you can't afford to have anyone dragging your party mood down!

If you aren't seeing enough plusses over your partygoers' heads, try having them gulp down some punch. When your Sim is drinking the concoction, you can have him or her encourage other Sims to join in.

Juggling Needs

Don't forget about *your* Sims' needs during the party. They still require Comfort, which is severely compromised in dancing, riding a mechanical bull, or doing most any other party activity. As mentioned previously, the hot tub is the best solution for your Sims to get comfort, not to mention Fun, Social interaction, and even a little Hygiene.

Maintaining the Mood

As the party progresses, keep an eye on that moose. If your resident Sims are happy but the overall mood remains low, focus your attention on Grumpy guests. Feel free to cut loose any Sim who is ranting with a red symbol in his or her bubble. These Sims are clearly unhappy, and keeping them around only hurts the party. Manage your own Sims, and make liberal use of the Join command. Pick group activities and drag the other Sims into participating. Spread your activities out over all of your party toys, but try to keep the toys in one place as much as possible.

Fig. 15-8. The hot tub is a surefire way to keep the comfort levels of your partygoers in the green.

Think of your resident Sims as a general indicator of the mood of the other Sims at the party. If your Sims are getting hungry, chances are at least some of your guests, are, too. Have them sit down for a bite to eat! Your guests will generally follow your lead, so long as they are in the immediate area. This is why it's a good idea to keep your party centered in one area of the house. Furthermore, Sims will waste precious time and energy walking if you've spread the party out all over the property.

> ## TIP
>
> *Espresso machines can really earn their keep at parties. Energy is the only nonrenewable resource when the disco ball is spinning, so a little shot of caffeine can be just the thing to help stretch your party into the night.*

Don't be ashamed to hire another Entertainer if you think your party could use a shot of fun. Also try dancing with several different partners over the course of the evening. If you pay attention, you'll find some Sims enjoy dancing more than others. Those that do will dance longer, and enjoy it more. Keep those Sims dancing with your own Sims until their Fun bar is glowing green. Outgoing Sims might even take a turn in the dance cages!

Fig. 15-9. It's a disco inferno!

Last Call

Eventually, your guests will start complaining about needs that they aren't getting fulfilled at your party. When you start seeing red complaint bubbles above your guests' heads, it's time to wrap it up. Start having your final chats with people, and then ask them to leave. The police will even come to break up your party if you let it go past 11 p.m., so don't let it drag on longer than it needs to. Bid your guests farewell, and then take care of any urgent needs your Sims have before sending them off to bed. Remember, your Sims skipped work the day of the party, so they need to make it tomorrow, or they risk getting fired!

Fig. 15-10. Lights out, and the place is thrashed. Good thing our Sims have a Maid!

Here is a general timeline of things to do before and during your party:

- ❑ **9:00am:** Have the Sim with the highest Cooking Skill cook up breakfast.

- ❑ **10:00am:** Engage your Sims in some sort of fun group activity.

- ❑ **11:00am:** Send your Sims off to the bathrooms for hygiene or bladder as needed.

- ❑ **12:00pm:** Have all your Sims settle in for an afternoon nap. While they are sleeping, buy all of your party objects (dance floor, DJ booth, etc.).

- ❑ **4:00pm:** Wake up your Sims. Take care of any urgent needs and call the Caterer.

- ❑ **5:00pm:** Make your first invite call.

- ❑ **5:30pm:** The party begins.

- ❑ **6:00pm:** Your first guests should be eating.

- ❑ **6:30pm:** Make your second invite call.

- ❑ **7:30pm:** Hire an Entertainer.

- ❑ **8:00pm:** Keep an eye on party mood and dismiss unhappy guests.

- ❑ **10:00pm:** Start dismissing your guests.

INDEX

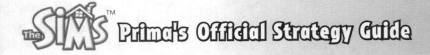

LEGEND

➕ **FIRST AID/SURGICAL TENT**

✖ **RESTAURANT**

👫 **RESTROOMS**

Prepare yourself for the most mind-blowing, stomach turning, heart-in-your-throat experience ever as you create and ride the wildest coasters imaginable. Build your ultimate theme park from a variety of worlds with over a hundred white-knuckle inducing rides and attractions. Then hop in a cart and feel the skull-crushing G-forces of your own coaster creations. Hire a staff, research new rides, and manage your budget to keep your theme park from going under. Let the battle between stomach and gravity begin.

www.SimCoaster.com

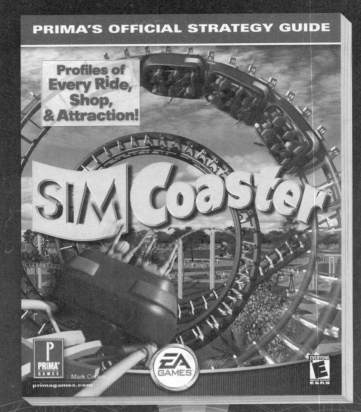